Stock Market for Beginners

How to Successfully Invest in Stocks, Guarantee Your Fair Share returns, Growing Your Wealth, and Choosing the right Day Trading Strategies for the Long Run

Peter Matera

Table Of Content

INTRODUCTION

The stock market seems a mystery, every now and then we hear about it in the news, we see it in movies, but most people are unable to understand how it really works and how it, in some way, holds the world together.

Much less is it easy to get how people use the stock market to generate income.

What is the stock market? How does it work? What do all those numbers and charts mean? How do people make money out of it? What is the easiest way to start making money out of it?

This book comes to answer these and every other question you could have about investments in the stock market in the easiest and most useful way possible, granting that at the end of the seventh chapter, you are actually ready to compete as a trader in the major markets of the world.

In the first chapter, you will have access to the theory, what is a trade and how the stock market works, including all the assets that are traded in it.

In the second chapter, we will show you how the prices move, how the contracts are managed and how you can calculate earnings based on the movement of the price.

In the third chapter, the technical part begins, and we will guide you through a step-by-step guide to understand the graphs and the way in which the market is measured.

Chapter fourth is when you get to see the advance part of trading, learning how to read the market through its patterns and figures.

Then in the fifth chapter, the math comes in, and you will learn how to use and even calculate simple, yet powerful, indicators that will make your life as a trader a lot easier.

In the sixth chapter, you will learn how everything is connected, and how your daily life has an impact on the market. Here we will show you how news can affect the price and trends and how you should behave as a trader when facing uncertainty and many other high-pressure situations.

Finally, in the seventh chapter, you will have access to three game-killing strategies that will allow you to dive into the market smoothly, and whose risk can be reduced greatly when combined with all the other tools that we gave you through this book.

Years ago trading was thought to be elitist, and not everyone could have access to it. But, nowadays, this has changed a lot, and you will now start a journey into one of the most wonderful fields of work that you can drive in.

Learn how the world moves, how money comes from one market to another and how assets fluctuate! A new world lies below this pages.

CHAPTER I:

Introduction to financial markets, raw materials, company shares, financial index, stock exchange, what is the stock market. Main stock exchanges of the World. Brokers Broker Regulatory Agents. What are ETFs and CFDs? What is the FOREX currency market?

• <u>Let's get started - Introduction to financial markets.</u>

The usual concept of the market is "a meeting of people in order to exchange a certain good or service" To begin with.

Nevertheless, this meeting must meet basic conditions such as the intention of groups of people to acquire a certain product or service and, in turn, another group with the intention of offering it.

In addition, the price of the product or service is a basic component variable.

This way, in the financial market, whose product is money, like any market meets its own basic conditions:

- On the one hand, there are groups of people or deficit companies, - those whose income in a period of time is less than their expenses-
- And on the other side are the surpluses, whose income is greater than their expenses, in that same period of time.

Both groups intend to exchange money through credit operations, and financial institutions act as intermediaries between them, channeling surplus groups through money placements represented in savings accounts, currencies, fixed-term certificates, and other securities.

Peter Matera

These money collections are oriented towards the deficit groups, through the issuance of promissory notes, credit agreements, credit cards, and other securities.

This way, the market price of money is the interest rate transacted in operations. And, without the existence of intermediaries, this price is transacted between bidders and claimants directly.

But usually, there will be a financial institution as an intermediary which will reserve a differential between passive rates, paid to surpluses, and the active rate charged to the deficit rate.

To put it simply:

In the financial market, operations close with a differential of price which represents the bidders and claimers income. If you open a 20 $ operation on an asset that grows to 30% of its value, your income will be of 30% of the value after closing the operation.

Yet, if there was an intermediary –Like a broker or a bank, which we will explain in detail later on- a difference will be held by them and deducted from your earning.

Note *– For an operation to be called successful, you should earn more than the risk factor + intermediary fees and transaction fees.*

• <u>What can I trade in the financial market?</u>

That financial market, where the majority of operations are for terms of less than one year, is characterized as a money market –When, for the most part, these operations are for a period longer than one year, we are in the presence of the capital markets.

In addition, the market in which foreign currencies are traded is known as the foreign exchange market –You've probably heard of it as FOREX-.

As in the financial market, everything moves through value, and there are many goods that can be traded allowing you to diversify any investment portfolio based on your knowledge and willing to take a chance.

Along the goods that you will find in the financial markets there are:

- Raw Materials.
- Actions.
- Financial Indexes.
- Stock Market.

Each one with their own characteristics and parameters –Including volatility- that you must keep in mind when you place your money.

Raw Materials.

In essence, a raw material is a natural resource that can be processed and sold.

This way, financial markets track, among others, agricultural products, metals, energy, and minerals.

Raw materials are the fundamental components of other manufactured products, both for industrial products, domestic products, and food.

These are distributed all over the world to meet demand because not all countries are capable of producing everything they need.

The production and consumption of raw materials depend on factors such as climate, season and resources, both natural and artificial which allows them to be relatively easy to read and to speculate with their price.

On the other hand, demand is also influenced by a complex interaction between economic factors and consumer habits which also influences the prices of raw materials to fluctuate considerably.

In general, raw materials are traded in very large quantities, in the spot market or, more often, in the futures market.

The raw materials can be grouped according to their common characteristics. See some of the terms used to classify them:

Agricultural raw materials

Generally, they are cultivated, they do not come from mining or extractive processes. Agricultural raw materials tend to be very volatile in the short term since they are susceptible to deterioration, which can cause their prices to wobble drastically and suddenly.

Producers try to get deeply involved in this market because they usually want to set prices for their products.

In combination with the natural growth cycle of these assets, this creates seasonal fluctuations in prices that usually follow standard patterns.

- **For example**, most people know that pumpkins and the stocks of companies related to their sales go high before Halloween

Other examples of these assets include corn, wheat, rice, sugar, oranges cocoa beans and livestock.

Mining raw materials

These are usually extracted from the soil or obtained from other natural resources.

The initial raw material can also be refined by obtaining some other product, for example, the oil is refined converting it into gasoline.

Some agricultural products, such as cotton, are also considered products from mining or extractive processes since they do not rot quickly and are industrial materials rather than food.

Products from mining or extractive processes are easier to handle and trade than agricultural products. They are more easily integrated into the industrial process which makes them a popular choice for investors.

In this regard, Oil is one of the highest grossing investment each year.

Other examples of mining raw materials are natural gas, aluminum, copper, silver, gold, and lead.

Emerging raw materials

There are raw materials that some investors expect to become booming markets in the future, but that is currently not available to operate due to their characteristics or legal aspects.

The only way to operate these products is through the stocks of the companies that operate with them.

Right now, the only examples of these are water and ethanol.

• <u>**Actions.**</u>

When looking to invest in the financial market, the second asset that you will find are the actions. An action is a unit of ownership in a company that can be put up for sale to possible investors.

These actions are measured when the total value of the company is divided into units of the same size.

If for example, if a company is worth 300 million dollars and issues 100 million shares, each share has a value of $ 3.

This way, when the value of the company fluctuates, the price of its shares move along with it.

Thus, investors who buy shares in a company have the hope that it increases in value, allowing them to sell their shares at a higher price in the future.

Buying shares directly can be risky, especially if the market in which the company develops is highly aggressive, seasonal or if the company is too new.

In other words, buying shares of companies that follow seasons, fight with claws and teeth for consumers or try to enter a new market poses a higher risk; yet, on the other hand, they turn out to be quite profitable if your prediction goes right.

An advice – Investing in actions usually goes only one way and is a direct buy/sale operation. But, if you have a good idea of which running actions can drop down in their price, you can go to the stock market and place money in selling operations to get earnings from that trend.

• <u>Financial Indexes.</u>

A stock index is a reference index that is formed with a set of securities listed on a stock exchange.

The indexes are created with baskets of listed and individual securities, which are called "constituent values of the index". It is very useful to analyze the price variations of several companies at a glance.

This way, a stock index is a numerical value, calculated according to the market prices of each of the securities that make up that index at a certain time.

Just like for most commodities, the profitability of an index is the variation of its value from one period to another.

But Indexes are not calculated just for investment, their main nature is to represent a measure, like a thermometer that serves to represent the evolution of the companies of a country, a certain sector of the economy or a type of financial asset.

The stock indexes that bring together the main companies of a country are an excellent indicator of the economy.

For example, these are the main stock indexes of the world:

- Dow 30, S&P 500, Nasdaq, SmallCap and S&P 500 VIX from the US
- Euro Stoxx 50 from the European Union
- S&P/TSX from Canada
- DAX from Germany
- FTSE 100 from England

Peter Matera

• <u>Functions of stock indexes</u>

The stock indexes can be used for many purposes, but mainly they:

Reflect the market sentiment.

Indexes serve as a benchmark to measure the performance of an asset manager.

Thus, allow comparing the profitability and risk that this manager has obtained with that of its benchmark.

It is worth mentioning that if the manager has two or more references in his investment universe this benchmark will be divided based on the value of the stock index that corresponds to each country.

Measure the profitability and risk of a market.

In addition, to reflect the behavior of the market, indexes allow us to review the risks of market operations in their given sectors.

For example, if you are looking to invest in foreign currencies –Which we will explain in more detail next in this chapter- like Euro, having a look at the European indexes, and indexes from their major contributing countries can get you to obtain information about how their markets are behaving.

This information is also useful to on-site investors and entrepreneurs who want to expand their companies to other countries or industrial sectors.

- **For example** – If you wanted to start an IT company, knowing how the technology index is working in the US can give you an idea about the right time to enter the market.

<u>***In addition, an index can be used to:***</u>

- Measure the beta of a financial asset.
- Create portfolios that mimic the behavior of the index.
- The basis for investment vehicles like ETFs, or financial derivatives.

Now that you know what uses the indexes have, let's take a look at how they are made:

How is a stock index built?

There are three main ways in which a stock index is built, these are weighted index price, weighted capitalization index and Equal weighting index.

Weighted price index: It is simply the arithmetic mean of the price of the securities that make up the index.

The advantage of this method is that it is very easy to calculate, but on the downside, stocks with the highest prices will have more influence on the value of the index, regardless of its real influence on the economy.

Two important indexes that use the weighted price method are the Dow Jones Industrial Average (DJIA) and the Nikkei Dow Jones Average.

Weighted capitalization index: it is constructed according to the market capitalization of each of the values that make up the index.

This type of indexes is the one that most faithfully represents the reality of what is going on in the market.

Most stock indexes in the world use this calculation method. As for example, the S&P 500 and the IBEX 35.

Equal weighting Index: These are calculated as the arithmetic mean of the profitability of each of the values that make up the index.

Peter Matera

It is not a widely used method since it is necessary to be continuously making adjustments and values with lower market capitalization have greater influence.

Two examples of indexes that use this method are the FT 30 and the Value Line Composite Average.

Where do Indexes come from?

Charles H. Dow was a great reviewer of the stock market and after observing that the actions of most companies fell or rose together, he decided to express the trend or level of the stock market in terms of the average price of a few shares representative

As in that time, the most representative companies were railway related, he made two indexes, one with the 20 most important railway companies and another with 12 shares of other types of businesses.

Important Indexes that you should consider when investing

There is practically an index for every imaginable sector of the economy and the stock market.

Some are known as 'major indexes', such as the Dow Jones Industrial Average, the FTSE 100, the S & P 500 or the Nikkei 225.

The leading indexes are provided by leading financial companies.

In this regard, the FTSE 100 is owned by the London Stock Exchange and the Financial Times, while the S & P 500 is operated by the financial heavyweight of Standard & Poors.

Higher rates provide a better evaluation of the performance of an industry, a sector or even the entire stock market of a country.

In Spain, for example, the Ibex 35 is the benchmark index for the national economy and brings together the main values of the Spanish stock market.

Types of indexes

An index can be defined based on the values that it represents into one of these three types:

1. World indexes
These include some of the largest global companies.

An example of this type of index is the MSCI World index, which measures 1,500 values extracted from each of the most developed markets of the world.

This index is often used as a reference point for funds.

2. National indexes
These indexes show the performance of the market of a specific country, reflecting the opinions of investors on the shares included in that market.

The FTSE 100 represents the 100 largest companies in the United Kingdom as included in the London Stock Exchange, on the other hand, the DAX does the same with German companies.

3. Sectoral indexes
These are more specialized indexes, designed to track the performance of specific sectors or industries.

For example, the Morgan Stanley Biotech index measures the top 36 biotech companies in the US.

Peter Matera

<u>**Other indexes**</u>

In addition to stock indexes, there are indicators for the other financial markets that affect the economy including:

1. **Currency indexes** – Which measure the value of one coin over other foreign currencies.
2. **Raw material indexes** - Like the Continuous Commodity Index which evaluates 17 commodity futures.
3. **Market sentiment indexes** - The 'CBOE (VIX) Index' measures volatility expectations in the short term, statistics derived from the prices of the S & P 500 shares.

How can I operate in an index?

You can't operate directly on stock market indexes, because they are not products by themselves, but rather indicators of market shares.

Instead, you can use derivative assets like CFD, options or futures which we will guide you through as we move on in this book.

• <u>Stock Market.</u>

The Stock Exchange is a market where plaintiffs and capital providers get in contact and carry out transactions through authorized intermediaries.

Many times you will hear people refer to it as "The Exchange".

Stock exchanges allow negotiation and exchange between companies that seek financing, and people or organizations who seek to obtain a return on their resources.

In stock exchanges, both variable income and fixed income are usually traded, and it is usually used to refer to equities since it is the most operated by individual investors.

The stock exchanges can be physical or virtual places that are managed by private organizations with the authorization of the corresponding governmental or regulatory entity.

Functions of the Stock Exchange

Given all the above, the stock market complies very specific functions among which are:

- Channeling savings to productive investment
- Providing truthful and permanent information about the values, the situation of the companies registered, operations carried out and other important data.
- Offering liquidity, since investors can convert their assets into money
- Provide legal security -the transactions are supported and certified by intermediaries and informational entities that will answer for them-.

In addition, stock exchanges have a fundamental role in economic development since they facilitate transactions and channel resources making possible a better allocation based on the market's real needs.

Advantages of the Stock Exchange for companies

Participating in the open stock market can bring several benefits to companies, among which are:

- Increased access to financing
- Clearer and a better image for the public

Peter Matera

- The possibility of estimating the value of the company at a given time and encouraging its administrators to increase that value
- Shareholders can obtain liquidity because if they wish they can sell their shares directly to the stock market at a clearer price

Advantages of the Stock Exchange for savers

People or entities that intend to save or take profit from the stock market can find the next benefits:

- More options to make your savings profitable
- Greater access to information
- Modify transactions as many times as necessary
- Access a regulated market that offers security

Where was the Stock Exchange Born

The stock exchanges come from the city of Bruges, Belgium where the family of bankers Van der Bursen organized meetings where assets were traded and commercial transactions were made.

The concept of "bag" arose from the family shield that had three leather bags.

The first modern stock exchange emerged in the year 1460 in Antwerp, Belgium followed by the London Stock Exchange in 1570. Later on, in 1595 Lyon, France and in 1792 New York came into play. The last one turning out to be one of the most important nowadays.

How does the stock market work?

The Stock Exchange is considered a secondary market since it transfers ownership of financial assets that have already been previously issued in the primary market.

The transactions here are carried out through authorized financial intermediaries known as popularly as brokers.

These agents are legal entities that act on behalf of the companies or individuals to carry out the transactions they deem appropriate and charge a commission or fee for their intermediation services.

It is worth mentioning that there are currently virtual stock exchanges where it is easy to contact a broker and buy shares in the online stock market.

On the other hand, companies that wish to participate in a stock exchange must make their Financial Statements public so that it is possible to obtain accurate information about their current situation and growth potential.

Main stock exchanges of the world.

The largest stock exchanges in the world could be classified based on several factors, such as the number of companies listed on the market or the market capitalization.

This way, based on the market capitalization factor, the ten main stock markets of the world are:

1. New York Stock Exchange:

Located: Wall Street
Established: 1792.
Current market capitalization: around 14,000 billion dollars
Market operation: from 9.30 am to 4:00 pm

Also relevant information:

- Physical purchase of shares is also available, although obviously, the transactions are mostly electronic.
- Large, medium and small capitalization companies are on the New York Stock Exchange.
- It was merged with American Stock Exchange in the year of 2008. The.

2. NASDAQ:

Located: New York

Established: 1971.

Current market capitalization: around 4.5 billion dollars

Market operation: between 9.30 am and 4 pm, including pre and post-market sessions from 07 a.m. to 8 p.m.

Also relevant information:

- Is the second largest stock exchange in the US.
- NASDAQ stands for National Association of Securities Dealers Automated Quotes
- Holds the same stock exchange in eight different European countries

3. Tokyo Stock Exchange:

Located: Japan

Established: 1878.

Current market capitalization: around 3,300 billion dollars

Market operation: between 9:00 and 15:00.

Also relevant information:

- TSE is the third largest stock exchange in the world and the largest among Asian countries,
- Has more than 2,000 companies listed.

- When this bag was introduced with new methods of the transaction in the year of 2005, it was severely affected by insects and closed completely for four and a half hours.
- This was the worst interruption in the operations that this stock market has suffered.

4. The London Stock Exchange:

Located: Paternoster Square, London
Established: 1801.
Current market capitalization: around 3.396 billion dollars
Market operation: between 8.00 am and 4.30 pm.

Also relevant information:

- This is the oldest international stock exchange in the world in which about 3,000 companies from 70 different countries are listed.
- Among European countries, this stock exchange has the highest value in the capital market.
- In 2011, it was publicly announced that it had merged with the TMX group. 3

5. Hong Kong Stock Exchange:

Located: China
Current market capitalization: around 2,831 billion dollars
Market operation: between 9:15 a.m. and 4:00 p.m.

Also relevant information:

- During the year 2011, this stock exchange was placed in the sixth position in terms of market capitalization.
- There are no strict controls on external investors.
- Is the largest stock exchange in China with about 1,470 companies listed.

- Initially, it was called the Brokers Association, but it was later renamed the Hong Kong Stock Exchange in 1914.

6. Shanghai Stock Exchange:

Located: China
Established: 1990.
Current market capitalization: around 2.547 billion dollars
Market operation: between 9.30 am and 3 pm.

Also relevant information:

- This is the third largest stock exchange in the Asian continent and the second largest in the People's Republic of China.
- not fully open to foreign investors with strict regulations issued by the China Securities Regulatory Commission.

7. Toronto Stock Exchange:

Located: Toronto, Canada
Established: 1852.
Current market capitalization: around 2.058 billion dollars
Market operation: between 9:30 to 16:00.

Also relevant information:

- Maintained by the TMX group of Canada.
- It is one of the largest stock exchanges in the world and the third largest stock exchange in North America.
- Several companies from Europe, Canada, and the United States are listed in this stock exchange.
- Leads in the mining and oil sector.

8. Deutsche Börse:

Located: Frankfurt
Established: 1971.

Current market capitalization: around 1,486 billion dollars

Market operation: between 8:00 and 22:00.

Also relevant information:

- It is one of the few stock exchanges that are involved with charitable organizations.
- Has about 765 companies listed on the market.

9. Australian Securities Exchange:

Located: Melbourne and Sydney

Established: 1861.

Current market capitalization: around 1.386 billion dollars

Market operation: between 9.50 am and 4.00 pm.

Also relevant information:

- They offer all products such as bonds, stocks or commodities among others.

10. Bombay Stock Exchange:

Located: Dalal Street (Broker Street), Bombay

Established: 1850.

Current market capitalization: around 1,263 billion dollars

Market operation: between 9.15 am and 15:30.

Also relevant information:

- Until 1874, the trade took place under the Bengal fig tree on the Mahatma Gandhi Road, Mumbai.
- More than 4,900 companies are listed on the Bombay Stock Exchange.

• <u>Brokers and their Function.</u>

By this point, you already have an idea of what the exchange markets are, where they are and how they work, so, it is time to get to know the intermediaries who will aid you in investing process.

Nowadays, brokers are platforms that work as intermediaries and are indispensable tools for investing in the stock market.

They are the global equivalent of agents or stockbrokers who in previous years were the only bridge between Wall Street and the common man –Keep in mind that old school brokers still exist, and you can actually call a bank or a broker agent and get transactions done through a physical intermediary-.

These platforms can be accessed from different parts of the world and their bases or physical offices are equally distributed around the globe.

Their job is to simply translate or execute purchase and sale orders in the different securities in exchange for a commission that varies from one platform to another.

Imagine their role as that of our mother when we were little children and we wanted her to buy something for us. She was our intermediary (broker) to be able to access (purchase order, in this case) to different kind of sweets (product) that is only a few children the cashier of the market (stock market) would not sell us-

The difference here lies in the resources, which now are yours and the option to sell the asset back to the open market when the price changes in order to generate earnings.

Thus, with the creation of these platforms, ordinary men and women from all over the world can take part in a more direct and conscious way of the market movements, and take advantage of it.

This way, to start trading and take your first steps in this world, the first thing you should do is create a broker account.

This process is at an intermediate point between registering in a social network and opening a bank account.

While it is very simple, as it is about money and the safety of users and the legality of the system is paramount; for this reason, you will always be asked to verify your identity before the institution.

In fact, if you get by a broker that does NOT require proof of your identity at any point, you may not be in the right place.

What differentiates online brokers from the traditional brokerage?

The difference is simple, they use the internet as a mean of communication with their customers and offer the possibility of a direct control over your current operations.

You can buy and sell securities, stocks, and products just as you would directly on Wall Street.

However, the vast internet and all its power allow anyone today to have a website opening the way to new and great initiatives as well as large-scale scams.

Therefore, you will find a large number of brokers online, some more serious and legal than others.

How do I choose the Online Broker that best suits my needs?

First, not all brokers are suitable for all types of investors – Especially if based on your capital investing power-

There are some whose minimum entry amount is $ 100 but the investment is $ 3000, forcing users to use risky leverage for their money.

Therefore, you should consider both the investment capital and the minimum lot to negotiate offered by the broker in question.

Then but definitely not less important is to ensure the legality and registration of the chosen broker.

Brokers regulatory agents.

A duly registered broker must submit a physical address in his platform, usually in the contact section or "about us".

In this sense, they must be registered or regulated by the corresponding agency in that country, which should also be indicated in the legal bases of the platform or in the frequent questions section of the same.

In addition, depending on the internationality of the site, other countries or regulatory entities of this type may require a relevant registration to work with residents of that country, regardless of whether their facilities are there or not.

Here are the acronyms and the country to which the most important regulatory entities that you should spot belong:

U.S:

- CFTC: Commodity Futures Trading Commission

- FINRA: Financial Industry Regulatory Authority
- NFA: National Futures Association
- SEC: Security and Exchange Commission
- SIPC: Securities Investor Protection Corporation

UK:

- FCA: Financial Conduct Authority

Eurozone:

- ESMA: European Securities and Markets Authority

Japan:

- JSDA: Japan Securities Dealers Association
- FSA: Financial Services Agency

Switzerland:

- FINMA: Swiss Financial Market Supervisory Authority

Germany:

- BaFin: Federal Financial Supervisory Authority

Spain:

- CNMV: National Stock Market Commission

France:

- AMF: Authority of the Financial Markets

Australia:

- ASIC: Australian Securities and Investments Commission

Canada:

- IIROC: Investment Industry Regulatory Organization of Canada

Peter Matera

Cyprus:

- CySEC: Cyprus Securities and Exchange Commission

Denmark:

- DFSA: Danish Financial Supervisory Authority
- FSA: Financial Supervisory Authority

China:

- CSRC: China Securities Regulatory Commission

Usually, online brokers work with comparative products that reflect the global feeling and price of the markets; this way you are not investing in the asset directly, but in a certificate or a contract which value is based on the price and the action price of the asset that you operate with.

There are called ETF and CFD.

• ETF and CFD

The ETFs or Exchange Traded Fund are investment instruments with which we operate in the same way as if we operated with an action.

It is a fund that can be sold or bought in units of shares, as easy as it is with an investment fund and the times that are required throughout the day.

ETFs are replicating at the same or lower scale of other assets or groups of assets.

These, agglomerate instruments of the same item so that investors can invest in all of them to purchase or sale without having to search one by one. For example, among the most quoted today we find:

- **AMLP**: Alerian MLP Infrastructure.
- **DBEF**: Deutsche X-trackers MSCI EAFE Hedged Equity.

- **DUST & NUGT**: Direxion Daily Gold Miners Bull and Bear 3X Shares.
- **JDST**: Direxion Daily Junior Gold Miners Bear 3X Shares.
- **QQQ**: Invesco QQQ Trust Series 1.

On the other hand, CFDs or Contract for Difference is financial instruments that bet and manipulate the price of an action, commodity, index, bond or asset based on an underlying asset.

When acquiring a CFD, you receive earnings based on the difference between the opening price and the closing price of your operation.

Here you may notice that the CFD purpose is to avoid having to access an action directly, but then following such action's reaction to the market investment.

In addition, with this type of contract it is possible to obtain gains both upwards and downwards of the market, which does not work in the same way in the case of real purchase contracts.

Operating with CFDs also gives you the possibility to manipulate the market price, which, in the case of real shares, Microsoft for example, are the clients of that company that give value and raise and lower the price directly.

Advantages of operating with CFDs:

- Earnings in both directions
- Ease of acquisition
- Affordable price
- Manipulation of the price by the Traders

Disadvantages:

- Trading market influences their price, but they can slow it down a lot if they make opposite decisions.

- Leverage with these investments is usually low, and so are your earnings.
- Although the purchase of a real share can generate huge profits in a few minutes, with the CFD covering only the movement during the operation, it will always represent a smaller amount.

Among your operative options in any broker, you will also find out a more volatile market, and probably the one in which you can generate most of your income as a trader.

• <u>Forex</u>

The Foreign Exchange Market represents the International Currency Market.

It does not belong to any political power, it does not have a main administrator body, nor is it manipulated by any particular government for convenience and in it, and the only operative product offered is money.

Forex represents the most liquid market in the world moving more than 5.1 trillion dollars per day through operations that are carried out via telecommunications 24 hours a day, starting on Monday at 00.00 GTM and ending on Friday at 22.00 GTM.

NOTE – The best time to participate is from 3:00 AM to 3:00 PM, New York time. This is because all European Markets open at 3:00 AM and the ones in America sum up later on allowing you to appreciate an almost worldwide picture during that period of time.

CHAPTER II:

What is a Pip or a Tick? Location of the Pip. What are the Lots? Leverage. MT4 platform installation and features.

• <u>The point, Tick, and pip</u>

Points, ticks and pips are the measures in which we tell how much the price changes in a given time, mostly looking at the opening and closing price on a given Japanese Candlestick —We will get to the candles later-.

Pay special attention to this point! The change in the price is where you can measure your earnings and losses, and the probability of an outcome when you open any trading operation.

Points

A point is the largest of the three terms, and it is the smallest possible price change on the left side of the decimal point of a quote.

For example, an asset may experience a price change from 1000.00 to 1001.00, which would be a price change of one point.

<u>*If gold (AUX) moves from 30.00 to 31.00, that is a point.*</u>

A point is composed of ticks, which are the price movements that occur on the right side of the decimal point of a quote.

Ticks

A tick is the smallest possible price change for the market in question, and it can be anywhere on the right side of the decimal point.

Differently, from the points, the markets have different sizes of ticks.

This way, shares that have a tick size of $ 0.01 move in increments of $ 0.01.

Futures markets also move in ticks, and the "Tick Size" varies according to the futures contract.

For example, some contracts have a tick size of 0.25, or in the case of gold futures, the tick size is 0.10.

To see the value of the tick of a futures contract, you have to look up the contract information in your broker's site.

The points are composed of the number of ticks that add a point when summed up.

But there is an even smaller price movement measure.

Pips

A pip is the smallest movement in the price that occurs in the fourth decimal place.

To put it simply, if the USD / CAD currency pair moves from 1.1000 to 1.0001, this is a movement pip.

The amount of money worth a movement of 1 pip is known as Pip Value and depends on the characteristics of the asset that you are operating in, which you can see in the broker's contract information of the given asset.

• <u>Lots, Mini lots and Micro lots.</u>

In FOREX, the amounts managed through CFD's is higher than the real deal, this happens because, despite the market's volatility, the movements are actually really low moneywise.

In other words, if the EUR-USD pair moves 50 pips in favor of the American coin, and you invested for that tendency based in 100$ you will get 0.0050 $ for each dollar invested... which is basically nothing.

For this reason, lots come in and create greater valued items, you will be then investing in a % of the lot instead of the equal of the money invested.

So, let's say that you bought a Lot of 100.000 $ through a CFD and at 1.3444 EUR, and then the asset grows out 20 pips –This would be 1.3464 EUR- the value calculated by Lots would be **(0.0001/1.3444)* $100.000 = $ 7.43.**

This way, $ 7.43 20 pips = $ 148.7 which would be your return.*

Calculate your earnings!

Just as we used it before, the formula to know how much an operation just gave you –Besides the fact that the broker will always tell you how much you earned- goes as follows:

1. *(DUV /IP)* LotV = EfDU*
2. *EfDU * NDU= Brute Operation Earnings*
3. *BOE – Broker's Commissions = Total Earnings*

Where:

- DUV: Differential Unit Value
- LotV: Lot value
- EFDU: Earnings for Differential Unit

- NDU: Number of Differential Units
- BOE: Brute Operation Earnings

Now, not all lots have a value of 100.000 units –Even when this is a standard measure- there are others known as Mini-lots which have a value of 10.000 Units of the asset and Micro-Lots which have a value equivalent to 1.000 units of the asset.

By knowing this, you are already aware of how to place your operations for the sake of greater incomes, most brokers also allow you to change the lot in which you are moving a currency, and this is good for either maximizing profit –With lots- or reducing risk –By using Mini or Micro Lots instead-.

Anyway, using lots is just a standard way to make the profit rate go up, and is approved by literally every broker, new or old that works with CFD's in FOREX.

But there is a way, which not every broker offers, or at least never in the same way, in which you can maximize your profits, **The Leverage.**

• <u>Leverage.</u>

The leverage is an option given by the broker that allows you to obtain great accessibility to the Market for a relatively small initial deposit.

This means that, if the market moves in your favor, your return may be much higher than in classic trading and your profits will, in consequence, be bigger.

On the other hand, it also works the other way around.

If the market moves against you, your losses may exceed your initial deposit, therefore it is very important to understand how to manage the level of risk when you operate with leverage.

For example, if you want to open an operation in EUR / USD of 0.1 lots, the value of the contract is € 10,000 and the leverage is 200: 1 or 0.5%.

This means that you would have to invest 0.5% of € 10,000, which is € 50, as a deposit to open such operation.

In other cases, you may want to invest in a CFD with a multiplier of 50, for example, and if such CFD exceeds your capital you won't be able to trade except for % or pieces instead of a full unit.

In these cases, leverage is also an option. If we say that you want to invest in DAX and the price of the contract is restricted to 1000 $, you could use leverage 100:1 to enter the market with 10 $ instead of having to deposit the full 1000 $ to be able to operate.

Said in other words, if you use a leverage of 100:1 you can actually invest in contracts with only 1% of the total value.

But as we mentioned before, leverage is a tough call, it poses a higher risk for every operation in exchange for the higher earnings offered, so, let's take a look to all the advantages and disadvantages of using leverage in your trading operations:

Advantages:

To begin with, Leverage allows you to optimize your investment by making it possible to trade long positions, compromising only a fraction of the value of the real transaction as initial deposit, but in addition, it allows you to:

- Take bigger positions than you could with physical purchases.
- Massively increase the return rate in proportion with your initial investment.
- Optimize your capital by investing in a wider range of different assets.

The risks of leverage:

As your profits increase, so your potential losses also grow.

You may even get to lose more than your initial deposit if you do not handle the risk cautiously.

To avoid the extra risks, most broker accounts allow you to minimize the losses by setting a guaranteed stop loss, this will close the operation when the price goes against you to a certain point –which you have to estimate- in order to protect you from a stronger devolution.

When available, this will limit your potential losses to a certain amount, but it also might close operations that can still be functional if you don't set it to the right price.

• <u>Mt4 platform. Features. Installation and functions.</u>

In this section about the MetaTrader 4 trading platform, you will explain you in a simple way and step by step how to download MetaTrader, how the platform is handled, the tools available to analyze the market and the basic concepts that you must know to open, manage and close operations.

Metatrader is a free investment platform developed by the company MetaQuotes Software Corp.

This platform, and especially its fourth version is mostly known as MT4, has become a Very useful and popular tool for investors around the world.

It's a Deep and complete platform, with a multitude of functions.

However, its handling is simple from the moment you know how the main elements work -which you are going to explain here- everything runs easily.

The objective is that you can learn to work through what is considered by a large number of operators as the best trading platform today.

WHY CHOOSE MetaTrader 4?

MT4 is the leading trading platform internationally.

The most used by traders of all kinds of profiles, strategies and experience level. It has a combination of factors, both for analysis and management of trading that make it unique.

In summary, to choose MetaTrader 4 as a platform to develop your online trading is a good idea for the   following reasons:

The user interface is attractive and effective.

It allows to easily organize all your workspace and the management elements of your trading business.

Is Flexible.

The platform offers multiple types of the configuration according to your preferences and changes applied to your platform customization can be saved, making it totally adaptable to any trader.

The graphs and analysis tools are complete and professional

It also offers a large number of technical indicators). Still, its handling is easy. It is suitable for traders of any level.

Is also compatible with numerous investment instruments

Including currencies, commodities, cryptocurrencies, stocks, stock indices

Peter Matera

It is suitable for all kinds of strategies of trading.

The   Execution and order management is simple and intuitive. Facilitating all the operations.

Is designed to use automatic trading systems.

Computer programs that are installed on the platform and are responsible for executing purchase or sale operations automatically according to a series of indicated parameters.

Working with an online broker that is tied to Metatrader 4   you have everything needed to trade.

This way, you can analyze the graphs, know the negotiation conditions, make the decisions and execute your operations from a single point instead of having to use different apps or programs.

Devices compatible with MT4

MetaTrader 4   is available for you to download for free on a desktop computer, laptop or on any mobile device, including smartphones and tablets.

You can also operate in the financial markets with this platform through its Youbtrader version using your browser and without needing to download and install the platform on any device.

On the downside, if you are using Linux OS, then you will have to settle for the Youbtrader version of the system.

Metatrader 4 Step By Step

If you are going to use a mobile phone or tablet you only have to download and install the app for iOS or Android.

It is a simple process and in a few minutes, you will have it ready.

In addition, the platform is quite similar and you can perfectly follow this guide to know all the options and possibilities that this tool offers you.

Next, you are explaining you step by step how to install and use the MT4 program in your Windows OS computer:

Step 1- Downloading The Program

You have two options when downloading the Meta Trader 4 trading program:

The first one is to search and download the app directly through the MetaQuotes Software Corp. website –the company that developed the programs.

But the second option is more advisable. You can perform the download through an online broker that offers this platform.

The brokers offer the same version, with the difference that you will get an associated trading account to be able to operate directly, and depending on the broker, there can be other advantages like demo accounts to practice your trading with 0 risk –And 0 earnings, of course-

The last is useful to gain experience in the markets before performing operations in real mode putting your money at risk. It is also a good tool to get completely acquainted with MetaTrader 4 so that you can learn to manage this platform with absolute confidence.

Having the platform associated with a broker facilitates the process to spend in real mode.

Peter Matera

Additionally, the broker automatically offers the evolution of the prices of financial instruments in real time along with additional services that the broker can offer like economic calendars, training, market analysis, and trading forums.

For this guide, you will be directed to use a platform like ActivTrades, XM, ESFBS, XTB, Pepperstone, FXpro, IG, HotForex, ICmarkets or Avatrade which offer MT4/5 accounts for you to enjoy freely.

After opening an account in any of the above-mentioned brokers, look for the MT4 demo account option in their website and you will be redirected to a screen with the registration form of the demo account:

Initially, the data requested is basic, your name, city of residence, contact information, and language.

Next, you must enter your preferences for the demo account, which includes:

1. Type of platform –Where you will select MetaTrader 4.
2. Account type –The demo account is a simulator of a real account, so just select standard and keep going.
3. The base currency of the account –Universally it is better to use USD as your main currency because almost every contract is based in USD and it will be easier for you to follow up the prices. On the other hand, you can go for your local currency if you feel more comfortable with it, the platform has dozens of currencies to show the accounts.
4. Leverage –Remember the monsters? Here you can choose a limit for your leverage, and even set up a base leverage that will be in your operations without you needing to call for it every time.
5. Amount of investment –This is the money that you are willing to put in the platform; since you are talking about the demo account, it can be whatever you want. However, it is advisable that you train with a number that is as close to your reality as possible, this way you will get used to investing based on your real capabilities.

6. Finally, enter a password, confirm it to avoid errors and press on the "Open Demo Account" button.

After this step, you will receive an email from your broker which looks for confirmation.

After a few minutes, the broker you selected will send a second email to provide you the Access data to the trading platform.

In this mail is where you will usually get the link to download the MT4 platform in your device.

Next, select the version of the program that is compatible with your computer, wait for the .exe file to download completely and start the installation process.

At the end of the installation, you will have an icon on the desktop to access the platform, although it starts automatically at the end of it.

First access –Usually automatic after installation

Here you will have to provide the information that you mentioned above, you recommend you to check the case that says "Save Personal Information". The reason behind this is that the password generated by the broker can't be changed, and is usually long and difficult to learn and input, which makes it better to just save it somewhere else in case of emergency but has it fixed in the program.

Congratulations! This far you already know the basics and have access to the trading platform. But the journey isn't over yet; in order for you to start trading, there is more than you need to know about this platform.

Step 2- How To Use It

The MetaTrader 4 is perfectly customizable, this is one of its advantages.

However, the first thing you should do is know the different elements of the platform.

Here we explain it divided in a section for each menu available:

Menu bar - This bar is in the top of the screen, is basically composed of the menu with the next options that we will explain:

Archive - From this option, it is possible to perform the most basic tasks of the account and the platform like opening a new chart or requesting a new trading account. It is also the place in which the configurations with the customization of the interface can be saved in "User Profiles". A profile is a personalized workspace within MetaTrader 4. You can create different profiles and upload them as needed.

Watch - From this section you can configure the workspace, adding and removing buttons, bars, asset visualization, and other elements.

Insert - This menu gives us all the tools that a trader usually adds to the stock chart on the occasion of developing his technical analysis, including, Indicators like ADX, Bollinger Bands, Stochastic, MACD, Mobile Media, Parabolic SAR; Lines to draw trend guidelines, Tools of Analysis of Gann and Fibonacci, Figures, Text tags and more.

Graphics - If the "View" menu was dedicated to the customization of the elements of the platform, this "Graphics" menu goes on the same line; only that it is oriented to the configuration and personalization of stock charts.

Here you can set the type of graph -change from candles, bars, lines-, colors, add elements like the background grid, selection of the temporary period, zoom, etc.

From the submenus " List of Indicators "and " Objects ", you can visualize, insert and eliminate all the technical indicators and other elements that are inserted in a certain graphic.

You are also able to save templates with a certain graphics configuration.

In this way, your set indicators, temporality and other elements belonging to a specific trading strategy, can be accessed through the "Template" submenu.

Besides, in the "Template" Submenu is a drop down to save, upload and manage everything related to the templates along with pre-configured templates that you will find really useful.

Tools - From this menu, it is possible for you to launch trading orders and carry out tasks such as Expert installation Advisors and control the general options of the platform.

In the "History center" submenu you have historical data to download for each asset chart.

You can use this information to perform "backtesting" and in this way to configure and optimize Expert Advisors.

Window - From this menu, you can configure the organization and visualization of the different windows. MT 4 allows you to display more than one graph simultaneously.

Good organization is fundamental for trading. Thus, you can open new windows, establish a mosaic, cascade, or vertical display; you can also organize the icons and select the graphic on which you want to work.

Help - This menu allows access to multiple help options with respect to the platform offered by the developer.

Buttons and icons under the Menu Bar - Under the bar of the above menu you have a series of buttons and icons that serve as direct access to several of the most frequently used options.

Many of them you have already seen within the different submenus above and from here you can access them more quickly.

You can customize all these elements adding others that you need or eliminating those that are unnecessary. For now, unless you have more experience, it's better to leave them by default.

Market Observation Window - This window shows the financial instruments in which you can operate and their current prices. You can insert and/or delete instruments at any time to leave it according to your preferences.

The information that this window offers is, in the form of a list, with:

1. The symbol of the instrument.
2. The price that the broker will offer if you want to sell the asset.
3. The price that the broker will offer if you want to buy the asset.

About the sale and purchase prices: when operating with Forex or CFDs, you can obtain benefits whether the price of the instrument goes up or down.

If you think the price will go up, you can open a purchase position to close it later with a sale and collect benefits.

On the other hand, if you think the price will go down, you can open a sales position and close it later with a purchase.

This way, you can take advantage of both bullish or bearish movements whereas if you physically buy the instrument you can only obtain benefits if you sell them after increasing their value. –As we explained the CFD's earlier in the first chapter of the book

The Price difference between Bid and Ask is what is called Spread. It is what the broker charges us as a commission for conducting an operation.

Normally, this price differential or Spread will be charged to the newly opened position. For this reason, all operations begin with a small loss until the price evolves in our favor.

The purposes of this window of observation of the market are surveillance, monitoring and being able to quickly operate the main instruments object of our operations.

In addition, you can add or remove the assets from the menu "View" and then "Symbols", as you have seen above if you right-click on them with your mouse.

Above this window, you have all the options for the management of both the window itself and the instrument that you have selected.

Browser window - This window has options to the following elements of the platform:

- Accounts: Visualization of the different accounts you have. Being able to change from one to another.
- Indicators: Complete list of all the technical analysis indicators that can be inserted in a chart.
- Expert Advisors: Selection and use of different Expert Advisors that you have been able to install.
- Scripts: Automatic instructions that are left configured to make our trading easier.

Graphics Window -From the graphs, you can analyze markets, insert indicators and execute orders directly on the platform.

To this, you can sum up the possibility to visualize more than one graph simultaneously. In this way the trader has the opportunity to control several assets at the same time; either for its monitoring and control or because it has open operations in more than one market.

If you click with the right mouse button over the window of some chart, you have all the options corresponding to its configuration, including the launching of orders to open a position and other functions related to the management of trading operations.

Peter Matera

The graphics can be closed, maximized and minimized. But to open a new chart you will have to resort to the menu or the window of Market observation, clicking with the right button on the corresponding asset of our list.

Remember that it is possible to save the configuration settings in a certain graphic on a template.

Terminal window - The main function of this window is intended to visualize and manage various functions related to trading operations.

- Operations: You have all the details of the operations in progress. Clicking with the right button in this window will show a drop-down menu that will allow you the complete management of the open positions.

- Exposure: is the total exposure to a particular financial instrument as a result of open operations.

- Account history: Allows to visualize the operations that have already been closed. Useful to get statistics and analyze our way of operating.
It is possible to obtain a complete report, with statistics included, if you click with the right button and select the corresponding option from the drop-down menu that appears –It says "Save as detailed report".

- News: Calendar or economic agenda. It is necessary that the broker has this service enabled.

- Alerts: From this tab, you can view, set and manage the alerts. An alert is a warning created by you for when the price of a financial instrument reaches a certain level.
As in all the tabs, if you click with the right button of the mouse the corresponding drop-down menu will appear that allows its configuration and management.

- Mailbox: It is simply notifications that the online broker sends you. In this case, they are newsletters related to trading and the platform.
- Market: These are different additional MT4 tools that are available for sale. From this tab you can directly access the market of the MetaQuotes community, in order to see their prices and if you find it appropriate to make the purchase.
- Signals: Service of trading signals from different traders that have more or fewer subscribers.
  They can be either free or paid and you can see the most general statistics of signal providers and set favorites. Any trader can be both provider and user of signals. You just need to be registered in the MetaQuotes community.
- CodeBase: In this tab, you have different Scripts, technical indicators and other additional tools to download that are usually published by MT4 users.
  You also have the option of ordering customized indicators and tools. All the information is published in the MetaQuotes community.
- Experts: These are files that contain all the information about the Expert Advisor attached. Such as the opening and closing of positions, messages, etc.
- Registration: As its name indicates, it is a journal-like record of the trader's actions during the current day.

The most used tab for taking and managing positions is that of "Operations". It is convenient to keep in mind the Terminal window and specifically this tab because it will be used to explain the different orders to manage the operation.

Step 3-Time to trade

Once you have checked out all the options that we mentioned above, trading will be very easy to start.

First, let's explain to you how to open an operation position:

There are four available ways to launch a purchase or sale order,

1. In the "Tools" menu, you click on the "New Order" submenu.
2. In one of the direct access buttons named "New order".
3. Directly on the chart. In the upper left corner, you have the direct function.
4. Right-Clicking on the graphics and accessing the drop-down menu Operations and New Order.

After going for any of those options, the corresponding dialog box to configure the parameters of the position you want to open will show up.

The elements of this dialog box allow you to establish a position adapted to the preferences, monetary management, and needs of the operation.

It is necessary then that you know how to open a position correctly:

Symbol: a Financial instrument in which the position is intended to be opened.

Volume: Size of the position. Expressed in batches or contracts –Remember the Lots we spoke about earlier?- It must be taken into account that this amount is divided between the leverage offered by the broker for that instrument and you will obtain the margin, or the amount that you must contribute as a guarantee to open the position.

Stop Loss: It is a fundamental risk control tool that allows us to specify a price so that the position closes automatically when reaching a certain value.

It serves to define a maximum level of loss that you are willing to support for this operation and therefore that the position closes if the price goes against us and this level is reached thus cutting the losses.

Take Profit: Order similar to Stop Loss, but this time it allows us to specify a price so that the position closes automatically when reaching a certain value. It serves to protect our benefits.

Comment: Allows you to attach a small comment or annotation about some factor that led the trader to open the position, or of any kind.

Type: You can execute the order to market, opening the position in the price in which it is at the time of executing it instantaneously; or establish a "pending order " which will enter the game at the position or price that you set.

After these, the table shows the sale price "Bid" and the purchase price "Ask" separated by a slash and the corresponding buttons to execute the order.

Buy: Open a purchase position, called a long position. In order for the financial instrument to appreciate.

Sell: Open a sales position, called a short position. With a view to the depreciation of the financial instrument.

After pressing one of these buttons the order will be executed and your position will remain open.

Step 4-Controlling your operations

The Open positions are displayed in the "Operations" tab.

They also appear in the chart of quotes of the instrument in which there are open positions. If you use the default colors of MetaTrader 4 you can see a yellow dashed bar and the Stop Loss and Take Profit orders are shown with a red dashed line.

In the Terminal window you will be able to spot the information listed below:

- Order: The order number assigned by the broker in order to identify said position with respect to others.
- Time: It indicates the date and time in which you open the position.
- Type: "Buy" or "Sell", depending on whether it is a purchase or sale order, respectively.
- Volume: The size of the position taken.
- Symbol: The financial instrument on which the operation is made.
- Price: The quoted price at which you entered the market.
- S/L: Price in which the Stop Loss order is configured.
- T/P: Price at which the Take Profit order is configured.
- Current Price: It is the price at which the financial instrument is in the present.
- Commission: Commission applied by the broker if it exists. About this, some online brokers offer lower spreads but in exchange apply a fixed commission per batch operated.
- Swap: It is a cost or commission that will be applied to obtain leverage and if the position is left open for more than one day. It represents the daily interest of the money lent to leverage your operation.
- Benefits: Benefits or losses of the open position. Depending on the evolution, the figure can be positive (benefits) or negative (losses).

Edit an Open Operation

A quick and easy way to edit an open position is by right-clicking or double-clicking on the dashed yellow line of the stock chart.

In addition to this path, you have the option to perform the same task from the Terminal window. Then, you must select the "Modify or delete order" command from the drop-down menu.

Whatever the chosen mechanism, after performing the action you will see a dialog box with the parameters of the open position that you can edit:

The dialog box is very similar to the one for opening a position but the parameters that you can modify to edit the order are only those corresponding to Stop Loss and Take Profit.

To do this you only have to edit:

- Level: A certain number of points, pips or ticks from the opening price of the position.
- Copy: Once the points in "Level" have been selected, you must press the figure that appears in this field so that the modification is recorded.

You can also set the exact price at which you want to modify the order by entering it directly in the fields corresponding to Stop Loss and Take Profit.

Finally, by pressing the lower button "Modify [order number and new parameters]" you will have the operation edited.

It is also possible for you to modify both Stop Loss and Take Profit prices by clicking and dragging on the graph the discontinuous red line that marks each of them.

Closing an operation

In the best and worst scenario, your position closes automatically if it reaches the value you have set for the Stop Loss and Take Profit parameters.

Either way, there are several reasons why a trader may want to close a position:

- If you find out an error in your strategy, is better to close the position before the stop loss plays along.
- The price has been turned against and the information highlights that it will reach the Stop Loss.
- The price cannot reach the level of the Take Profit and is preferably to close the operation manually before it in turns back.

Following that idea, to close off the position, the easiest way is to press the "X" that appears in the line of the open position of the Terminal window. This "X" is located on the far right, next to the "Benefits" monetary figure.

The same result will be obtained if you right-click in the position line and select "Close order" in the drop-down menu.

On the other hand, if you select the same dialogue box that you have seen to open position or edit it, having selected in the Type the "Execution by the market", in the lower part of the box you have the corresponding button to close position.

Partial Closure?

To carry out a partial closure you only have to modify the size of the position you intend to close in the "Volume" field. For this, you must access the previous table.

For example, if you have opened an order of 1 lot or contract, and decided to close the half, you will have to modify the "Volume" to 0.5 lots or contracts.

In this way only the selected volume will be closed, leaving the position with the remaining size open.

To sum up

MT4 allows you to edit, modify and create as many transactions as you need on the preferred markets. If you decide to open a demo account as recommended at the beginning of this section, you will be able to practice risk-free operational trading, which will allow you to gain the experience and knowledge that is needed in order to succeed in this field.

Following up, we will get you through what it means to make a technical analysis of the charts, including the reading, lines, tendencies, and candlesticks, which will give you a clearer path towards every investing decision.

CHAPTER III:

Introduction to Graphic Technical Analysis. Types of Graphics.

We already went through what happens in the charts and nice apps to use review them.

But now, is time to talk about what you will do with all that information.

Technical analysis is considered the study of market behavior as such, which means that all the information regarding the benefits and expectations of an organization, the sector to which it belongs, the economic, social and political environment, is reflected in the price of the title and, therefore, it is the market itself that offers the best information about the future evolution of the same.

Now, the market price of a security is determined only by the existing interaction of supply and demand, affected in turn by various factors, of a rational or irrational nature.

Where, all the economic information, including all the fears and hopes of the operators, are reflected in the price.

Therefore, technical analysis is the one that provides the only mechanism or tool, which allows measuring the irrational (emotional) aspect in the markets.

In this sense, it can be said that the technical analysis tries to identify the possible tendencies that begin to be drawn and to operate in favor of them. Being, another of the objectives of the technical analysis, to determine the moment in which the tendency begins to change.

Almost all the figures generally show, the mood or psychology both bearish and bullish investors. Given that the price discounts everything, it reflects, in turn, the fears and fears of the market and the expectations of the thousands of investors that form it.

Then, the technical analysis allows monitoring, analyze and make long and short entries in a large number of markets and values, without knowing in detail its economic fundamentals.

Technical analysis *– can be defined as the set of techniques (graphics and quantitative) that try to predict in some way, everything concerning the future evolution of prices based on their historical behavior, however, It is also made from some measurements such as volume and open interest.*

It is worth mentioning that graphics are the results that money leaves, given that they do not lie and you have to learn to trust the information and its story.

So, you have to learn to combine knowledge with self-control.

Therefore, the technical graphics analysis consists of learning when you must sell, buy or close any operation with the purpose of protecting it.

This chapter deals with the subject referred to the technical analysis of graph, chart types, times, Japanese candlesticks and lines: Support, resistance, preliminaries, levels, and channels, as well as market phases that you need to know in order to create profitable operations.

• __Introduction to Technical Analysis (Action Price).__

The technical analysis bases its predictions on the meticulous study expressed in the graphs that show the prices, tendencies and different patterns that the price is forming in the graph through its story.

On the other hand, it takes into account a considerable proportion of factors, such as price, trading volume, market volatility among others.

Being, the most relevant difference that it has regarding the analysis, is that it does not ponder aspects as related to political events, catastrophes, or other data, because all the information contained is taken from the price.

In addition, it studies the forms, figures or patterns that the price repeats and the results they offer in order to know what the price is most likely to do in the future.

One of the advantages offered by technical chart analysis is the ability to adapt to any type of financial instrument and any framework in which it operates.

Therefore, the techniques mentioned in the technical analysis can be applied to any type of price chart, whether you are working in the forex market, trading or if you are applying to binary options systems.

• <u>Types of graph Temporalities (Diffraction)</u>

A chart is a chart that represents the evolution of the prices, both of the markets and of the companies, of the financial assets, of the currencies, indexes, financial derivatives, investment funds. It is important to mention that on the vertical axis of the chart the quotes or prices are located and on the horizontal axis the time is indicated, that is, the trading sessions, be daily, weekly, monthly.

The purpose of the graphical analysis is to determine in what situation the quotes are and to try to predict what their future evolution will be based on their past evolution or graphic history.

The types of graphics temporality vary, according to their term, because they can be constructed with intervals of a few minutes, hours, days, weeks, months, quarters, years, being the most common the following:

The intraday charts:

Those that are built in periods shorter than the duration of the trading session, and may include intervals of ten, fifteen, thirty minutes. Also, you can build intraday graphs of lines, bars, candles.

The daily charts:

Are those that are built with the daily variations of prices or quotes

The weekly charts:

They are graphs constructed with the variations of the prices or weekly quotations of a value or market. Allows vision and decision making in the medium and long-term

• __Japanese candles. Types of candles and Candle patterns.__

Japanese Candlesticks are a technique that began to be used for several centuries ago in the rice market in Japan, and from there has been extending to other markets and countries.

Peter Matera

They can be used in any chart of any asset being the most common: stocks, commodities, currencies and at any time scale (graphs, monthly, weekly, daily).

The importance of Japanese candles, is that they provide clear and fast information, particularly about how the Price and market psychology has been during a time period, if it went from more to less or less to more, if despite the volatility things ended as they started and if there were inner tendencies that didn't match the final result.

They are also better at indicating where the fall or rise in which we are immersed in each moment could end, give way to a new trend.

This point is very important and turns them into a very good complement to the technical analysis since the figures of the Japanese candlesticks warn before the floors and ceilings of the market that the figures return from the technical analysis.

Each session, or period, is a bar, or a Japanese candle.

A period can be a session (a day), or a week, a month, a year, an hour, 30 minutes. Both the technical analysis bars and the Japanese candlesticks are drawn with 4 data:

1) Opening price of the period
2) The closing price of the period
3) The maximum price of the period
4) Minimum period price

Shadows are also important because when the maximum of a session coincides with the opening or closing price of that session, there is no upper shadow. And if the minimum of a session matches the opening or closing price of that session, there is no lower shadow.

On a daily chart, each candle represents a period of one day; in a graph per hour, each candle represents one hour, and so on. Below, a visual analysis of the candle is presented:

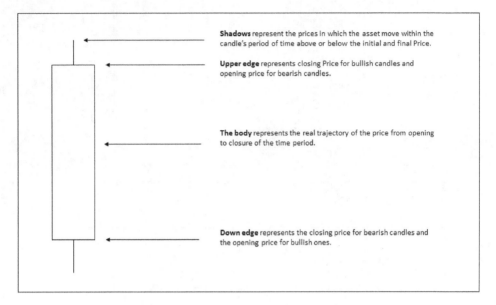

Shadows represent the prices in which the asset move within the candle's period of time above or below the initial and final Price.

Upper edge represents closing Price for bullish candles and opening price for bearish candles.

The body represents the real trajectory of the price from opening to closure of the time period.

Down edge represents the closing price for bearish candles and the opening price for bullish ones.

Candle patterns

Japanese Candlestick patterns

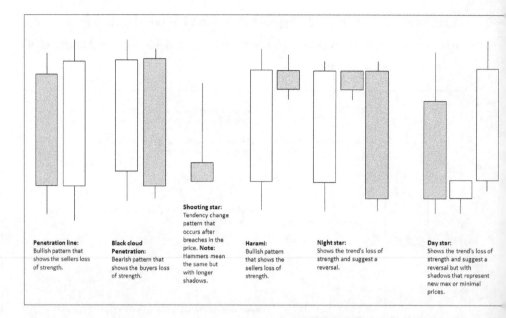

Penetration line: Bullish pattern that shows the sellers loss of strength.

Black cloud Penetration: Bearish pattern that shows the buyers loss of strength.

Shooting star: Tendency change pattern that occurs after breaches in the price. **Note:** Hammers mean the same but with longer shadows.

Harami: Bullish pattern that shows the sellers loss of strength.

Night star: Shows the trend's loss of strength and suggest a reversal.

Day star: Shows the trend's loss of strength and suggest a reversal but with shadows that represent new max or minimal prices.

It should be noted that when these patterns appear in a graph and when they appear at levels that coincide with other indicators, such as the Fibonacci retracement levels or the moving averages, a potential purchase-sale opportunity is created.

Important Candle Patterns

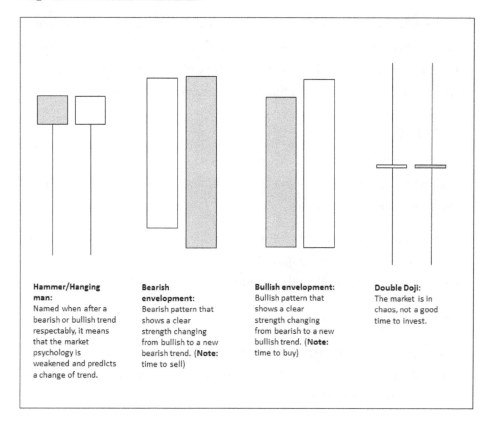

Hammer/Hanging man:
Named when after a bearish or bullish trend respectably, it means that the market psychology is weakened and predicts a change of trend.

Bearish envelopment:
Bearish pattern that shows a clear strength changing from bullish to a new bearish trend. (**Note:** time to sell)

Bullish envelopment:
Bullish pattern that shows a clear strength changing from bearish to a new bullish trend. (**Note:** time to buy)

Double Doji:
The market is in chaos, not a good time to invest.

Other useful patterns

Doji Bullish

Is considered a bearish trend indicator, where the market strengthens sellers with a long red period. However, the second period fluctuates in a very close range, and closes at or very close to its opening price.

This scenario generally shows a possible reversal, since many positions have changed. A confirmation of the change of trend would be a green candle in the following period of operation

Bullish Envelope

In defined as a bearish trend, the envelope candle opens at the closing price of the previous candle or in a new low and closes at a price equal to or higher than the opening price of the previous period. This means that the bearish trend lost its momentum and that buyers are gaining strength.

Hammer

After the market opens in a bearish trend, a marked oversold occurs. However, at the end of the period of operations, the market closes at or near the highest price of the period.

This means that the bearish sentiment is weakening, especially if the body of the candle is green. The change in trend can be confirmed if the next candle closes at a price higher than the opening price.

Harami Bullish

Then, from a long red period at the end of a bearish trend, a green candle opens at a price equal to or higher than the close of the previous period. The reversal of the trend will be confirmed if the next candle is green.

Doji Bearish Star

In an uptrend, the market strengthens with a long green period. However, the fluctuations of the second period occurred in a tight range and the price closes very near to the opening. This scenario generally shows the loss of confidence in the current trend. Confirmation of this trend would be a red candle below.

Bearish Envelope

In an uptrend, the envelope candle opens at the closing price of the previous period or at a new high, followed by a lot of sales volume, until closing at a price equal to or lower than the opening price of the previous candle. This means that the uptrend has been hurt and that sellers may be gaining strength.

Hung Man

After the market opens in an uptrend, an oversold occurs. However, at the end of the period, the market closes at or near the highest price of the period. This means a possible change of trend. A red candle would then confirm the change in trend.

Shooting Star

The market achieves a new high but can not hold it and the candle closes near its lowest point. This means a possible change of trend. A red candle would then confirm the change in trend.

Bullish Day Star

In a bearish trend, the market strengthens with a long red candle, but in the following period, the prices fluctuate in a tight range. This scenario shows a possible change in trend. The confirmation will be given with a green candle.

Bearish Black Cloud Coverage

In an uptrend, the candle opens strongly but loses its momentum to close to the middle of the previous candle's body. Black Cloud Coverage suggests an opportunity for sellers.

Bearish Sunset Star

In an uptrend, the market is strengthened with a green candle. However, the second-period changes and closes with a small red candle. This scenario shows the loss of confidence in the current trend. The confirmation of this change of trend is a red candle in the following period.

Peter Matera

• <u>Lines: Support, resistance, tendency, preliminaries, levels and channels.</u>

Now, candlestick patterns are not spotted so easily, and even when you see one, the usual is to confirm with the study that you have made over the historic and current trend in the first stages of the process.

This means that you need to know where the market is going in general, using the temporalities that we spoke about earlier.

Below are the supports and resistances, which are areas in which many have bought and sold -for each action that is purchased there is always another action that is sold, which are actually the same actions.

Some have succeeded and others have been wrong, and the memory of those past successes and failures influences the future behavior of investors when prices return to that area.

The supports are below the current Price or range, and the Resistances are above the current them.

The supports and resistances are one of the basic concepts of graphic analysis.

<u>About support lines</u>

A support in a bearish trend is a price level in which there is a break or rest in its bearish evolution, that is, a price level where the demand manages to be higher than the supply and, consequently, the fall of the prices.

The supports can anticipate bounces to the rise, in principle, in the short term and, therefore, reactions against the dominant bearish direction, continuing, once the bounce, the movement to the downside.

Therefore, a support provides, on numerous occasions, a short-term purchase signal.

A support level exceeded or broken down indicates that the supply has exceeded the demand and, therefore, that prices may continue to fall, at least in the short term, and until they find a new level of support.

So, the break it down, a support level:

- Provides a sales signal, at least in the short term, and depending on the importance of this level of support, even in the medium or long term.
- The breaks down support levels can be done with a high volume of negotiation of securities or without it, but in many cases, the second situation occurs, because as they say at the stock market prices fall by themselves.

The other side of the story: resistance lines.

A resistance in an upward trend is a price level in which there is a stop, slow down or rest in the escalation of the same, that is, a price level where the supply manages to be higher than the demand and, therefore, stops the rise in the price.

The resistances can anticipate a correction to the downside, in principle, in the short term, then continue with its main movement upwards.

Therefore, it is, in principle, a sign of a short-term sale.

The upward break of a resistance: is a level of resistance broken or surpassed to the upside, indicates that the demand of titles has surpassed the

Peter Matera

supply and, therefore, that the prices can continue rising, at least in the short term, and until find a new level of resistance.

Consequently, and depending on the importance of the resistance, the upward break of a resistance level provides a signal of purchase in the short, medium or long term.

The resistances broken upwards should be made with an increase in the negotiated volume; otherwise, it may indicate that the break is not reliable and that the price could go down again.

Below, is an example of how these lines should be drawn in you chart:

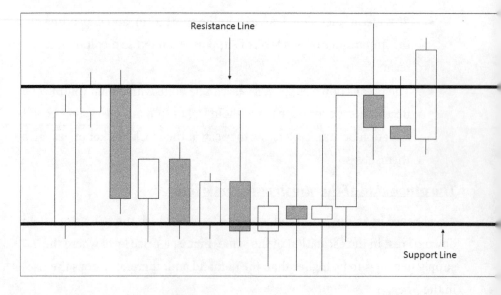

The tendencies or trends of the values:

The tendency is referred to the direction or trajectory in which the quotations of the values or markets evolve in time.

This price direction can be ascending, descending or flat, taking into account that, in most cases, we can define a bullish or bearish trend and, sometimes, a lateral trend.

Therefore, it can be noted that a trend is bullish, bearish or lateral as the following aspects concur:

- A trend is bullish when the successive supports and resistances are increasingly higher.
- A trend is bearish when successive supports and resistances are increasingly low.
- A tendency is lateral when the supports and resistances move laterally, without direction.

The drawing or drawing of the trend lines.

An upward trend is drawn by drawing a straight line that inclines at least two supports or ascending minimums This line is called the uptrend line that acts as a price support line.

Once the line is drawn, it will continue into the future, so that, as long as a market or value is in an upward trend, it must be operated in accordance with this situation, that is, acquisitions can be made or hold the securities in the portfolio.

The considerations that can be made of the Channels are the same as those of the trend lines, with the «addition» of the parallel line.

- The uptrend line is the base or floor of the Canal, and the parallel is the roof of the Canal.
- The floor is a purchase area, and the roof is a sales area, as it acts as a Resistance.

With the difference that as the Canal develops, the clearest selling area is the roof of the Canal, but less clear buying zone is the Canal floor, for what we said when talking about the uptrend lines. The trend lines are not infinite, and the more they develop, the clearer they are, but the less they have left to change to a lateral or bearish trend.

In case you have doubts, the software you use will draw you a perfectly parallel line where you set it so that you don't need to be skillful drawing. And in the end, your trend lines should look similar to this:

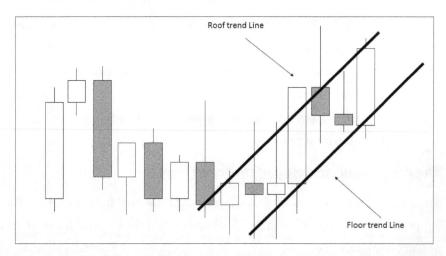

We could say that the line that could be drawn halfway between the ceiling and the floor of the Canal would be the «fair» value that the market assigns to that action at that moment, because in a very short term channel of an overvalued company or understandably, the «fair» value of that action is very far from that Channel

Logically, the floor channel would be the underestimation zone, and the ceiling would be the overvaluation zone.

That is, the wider a channel is, the stronger the trend. The narrow channels are the result of indecision, neither buyers nor sellers have a very different opinion from the opposite side, and anything can cause the channel to break easily.

Also, the wide channels end up breaking for one place or another, but they are more stable because they are created by more «grounded» postures, for whatever reasons.

Now, using these lines you can evaluate and mark your chart with the current market phases, which will allow you to get a bigger picture of what is happening with the price and therefore have an easy way towards the future possibilities.

This way, the next section is about the market phases, how do they work and how to define them.

• <u>Market phases.</u>

It is important to mention that before investing in any asset, you have to know in which market phase you are. This is because there are 4 main phases, and depending on which one, you will determine if you have to look for opportunities to buy, or to sell, or not doing anything at all.

At first, it will not work, but over time, the analysis is done very quickly and allows us to invest with the trend in our favor.

These four phases are given in all the temporary spaces that you can imagine, from monthly, weekly, daily or intra-daily graphs.

PHASE 1

This phase is reached after a prolonged period of a downward trend. During such a bearish, clear and long-lasting process, sellers have controlled the market, but now the price begins to move in lateral ranges, forming a base.

The selling force has been decreasing, and the confidence of buyers has increased.

Peter Matera

The market is in a balanced situation. Even so the perception that investors have on this market is bad, nobody trusts, there has been much suffering during the downturn, and even those who buy do so under an opportunistic profile, and not so much out of conviction.

PHASE 2

In this phase, the market leaves the lateral range in which it was sunk and the upward trend begins.

Although it is the clearest impulsive phase, its beginning is loaded with distrust, caused by the previous downtrend, and therefore many investors are determined to use the movement to sell, as if a bullish correction, and not a new one.

The fundamentals that make the market go around are not clear.

Sometimes it is caused by the simple stagnation in the deterioration of the situation. By the time most of the market sees that the improvements are evident, phase 2 is already well advanced.

PHASE 3

This phase is equivalent to phase 1, only that it occurs after a prolonged upward trend.

Buyers during this phase are those who have denied part of the course of the previous phase (the 2). These investors, who are now convinced that the market looks good, try to convince themselves that the lateral movement in which the market has been delimited now is only a stage of consolidation to keep rising.

However, the investors who bought at the start of phase 2 are already selling their positions. There is a balance between demand and supply.

PHASE 4

When the lateral range starts to break down, most investors perceive the movement as a mere correction, when in fact a new downward rotation has started.

The environment is favorable, with positive news even, and low perception of risk. That is why it is difficult to think that the upward process has ended.

The normal thing is that one realizes late that the current position is a bad one, and lose some of the previous earnings if a good part of phase 4 has already passed.

You should try to be active at the beginning of phase 2 (buying), and at the start of phase 4 (selling).

During phase 1 we will use to close sales, and during phase 3 to close purchases. It does not matter if once the positions are closed, phases 1 and 3 are extended, and we do not have positions for a while. The idea is to try to operate in favor of the trend because do not forget that the market, even in trend, suffers setbacks (corrective waves), and it is always easier to operate in favor of the trend.

CHAPTER IV:

Graphic Patterns and Chart Figures.

You will find the graphic patterns commonly in the financial market, basically are the graphic representations of the prices and changes.

That being said, with their help you can identify the easier way in which the price is going to move through the evolution of the market, including fluctuations of the price.

In the graphic figures there are two types of classifications with different implications for each one: the figures of **change trend**, which help you distinguish when there may be a change in the current trend, and **trend continuation** patterns, which indicate that the current trend will take a break, but still continue with force in a short term.

Take these figures seriously, as it has been shown that after these patterns the market tends to behave in a certain way.

This, allows you to predict how the market will respond to the current situation.

Note: There are even traders that consider figures and patterns to be enough to trade, and follow them blindly, using no other tool to measure the market.

Identifying these patterns is a talent acquired by the traders, it takes dedication and time to reach the competition, and acquire the greatest benefits of the future operation.

However, there are some programs on the web that can help you find them on the charts.

• **Continuation patterns:**

Continuation patterns will be one of the most useful tools that you can use since these will reflect the possibilities of a continuation of the current trend in the market, the fact that you can recognize these specific patterns will be of a great help to get the most out of and benefits from the operation

In short, the pattern of continuity is generated during a break from the dominant market trend, thus generating a lateral movement of price consolidation.

Despite being the most common patterns, these tend to be unreliable because of the short duration in time with which they tend to form and present, after a lapse, these will later return to resume the movement in the same direction of the trend of which they came

This way, among continuity patterns you will find:

Ascending Triangle:

This type of figure will help you to distinguish when there is a lateral pause in an upward trend that at some point will continue with your direction.

In short, it is the right time when buyers become more "wild" than sellers.

The ascending support line is formed by the minimums, this indicates that the sellers are starting to leave all their assets.

The upper horizontal line is formed by the maximum, this represents a resistance, which is what prevents the price increases, and this indicates that it is only a break and not a depletion of the trend, so while the formation of the triangle develops pressure from buyers will increase.

Symmetrical triangle:

This pattern will be of great help when distinguishing when there is a pause or lateral rest of the price in the market, the symmetrical triangle can be considered as a young trend which still has a formation and trajectory ahead.

This is the same for both bullish and bearish tendencies and does not usually have specific variations in terms of graphics.

Within the triangle, the price tends to vary or in this case "move" forming a Zigzag.

Descending triangle:

We cannot ignore the formation of descendant triangles, especially because it is a continuity pattern that usually appears in bearish tendencies.

It is a formation that pauses the movement of the market, thus generating a lateral consolidation, to then resume the movement in the same direction as the trend from which it came.

The name of this formation is due to the fact that it generates a line pointing to a bearish direction.

Inverted triangle:

Pay a lot of attention to the following figure, the formation of the inverted triangle is a repetitive pattern in the price that causes a lateral pause of the current trend.

It aims to give continuity to the current trend.

This pattern has destroyed the account of less professional traders, although it is not usually one of the most repetitive in the graphics, curiously turns out to be one of the favorites of the traders who like to take risks when the market price makes erratic movements.

This one is difficult to detect and unlike the other figures mentioned above, is usually a rare figure, it has the vertex at the beginning of the formation that generates its characteristic cone shape.

Flags:

A flag pattern is one of the most repetitive and most important figures when confirming the entries and thus obtain much more successful operations.

You will find it in the graphs of different temporalities as it indicates a continuity in the current feeling of the market.

Like any other pattern of continuity, this is a pause in the form of lateral consolidation that the price requires to continue its current direction.

This way, it does not have such a complex structure, its name comes from the physical figure in which the quote performs a movement in the form of a rectangle that points in the opposite direction to the trend, despite being one of the most important patterns, this is characterized by its simplicity.

Wedges:

This is a very classic pattern formation in technical analysis, as well as triangles or flags this indicates a continuity of the trend.

Its name is manifested by its characteristic features of a wedge, which is due to decreasing and distant minimums, and maximums that do not descend as quickly, the same way is if it is an ascending wedge

• __Return patterns: Enveloping candles, shooting star__

On the other hand, there are patterns formed by both lines and candles that show an almost secure change in the direction of the price.

Some of the candlestick patterns were mentioned before, and you will find here how they actually work in the open market.

In this section we will cover the most important ones:

Surrounding candles:

They are Japanese candlestick patterns, these will be of great help to distinguish when there is a change in the trend, and most professional traders consider them the ones with greater reliability.

So that this pattern can be fulfilled in the Japanese candles, it must comply with a basic rule, two (2) Japanese candles are necessarily one after the other, and the second one "will wrap" the body of the first one, hiding it completely.

This commonly happens when the price is marked in historical figures either by sellers or buyers, mentioning this, there are two types:

Bullish Envelope: You will find it composed by a first small bearish candle, and next to it a second much bigger bullish candle which will cover the whole body of the previous candle, which is preceded by a tendency previous bearish Traders use this pattern as a great opportunity to buy.

Bearish Envelope: This consists of the first small bullish candle and a second much larger bearish candle which covers the entire body of the previous candle. This is preceded by a previous uptrend. This can be interpreted as the sellers have taken control of the market, this is observed by the size of the candle, and that is, the sellers have set in motion a significant selling force.

Shooting Star: It is a pattern that consists of a change of trend formed by a candle, which according to the traders has a low to moderate reliability.

This pattern occurs during the bullish movements in the financial market, it gives us warning of a possible turn or change in this upward trend, which obviously changed to a bearish trend.

This figure can be distinguished by having a small body and black color, whose lower wick is small or nonexistent and the upper wick is at least 2 or 3 times the body of the previous candle, adding the indecision of the market to its closure at the end of the period.

It must be clear that value will always start with the force on the closing of the time before this, this figure is a pattern that always appears in bullish trends.

• __Chartist figures: Triangles, pennants, and channels. HCH, Double Ceiling, Double floor, Triple ceiling, Triple floor.__

Reference is made to the graphic way of being able to anticipate the evolution of future movements in the financial markets, as well as the values that comprise them. They consist of analyzing the pattern or figures of the graphic representations that make up the prices of the shares as an indication of the current trend and thus follow it in the shortest period of time.

Triangles:

You can usually find them as patterns of continuity, although sometimes they act as patterns of change. The minimum requirement so that a triangle pattern can be formed in a graph is that there are at least four points:

Two (2) for the upper line and another two (2) for the lower line, the really important of these patterns are in the direction they can move in the market and even more when the price breaks the triangular formation.

Peter Matera

Pennants and channels:

A pennant is one of the easiest and simplest chartist formations that exist, you will be able to detect it almost immediately when observing the graphs of the financial markets, it is one of the best options to carry out your operation. The pennant represents a lateral consolidation in the price, it is a few words is a pause before a movement in the direction of the current trend, it is a pattern of continuity, when you have the ability to identify them immediately you will see pennants everywhere in the graph, literally you will not be able to stop seeing pennants is one of the most repetitive and common patterns with which you can meet.

Shoulder-head-shoulder:

Shoulder-Head-man or SHS is one of the best known among all the formations for the most experienced traders.

You can find in the technical analysis, and despite being one of the most known most novice traders, tend to fail to try to effectively operate this figure.

It represents a change in the current trend that you may be following;

Keep in mind that there is nothing more unpredictable than the market if you try to bet everything on this pattern

His name is given by the shape that it presents, the first maximum forms the left shoulder, the second that exceeds the first would be the head, and the last one would end fixing the future market movements of the right shoulder.

Double roof:

This pattern means in most cases a change in the trend, you can also find it with a reversal figure.

It has a difference from those that have been studied before in this chapter and will help you to distinguish when you end a current trend and thus start a different trend, it is a change in the movement of graphs in the financial market.

The name is given to this pattern for its unique way in which it will help you distinguish two (2) maxima located almost on the same level as if they represent an invisible ceiling, which is not allowed to increase even more the price.

Double Floor:

This one is the opposite structure of the double roof pattern, there is not much to say about this figure only that they are governed under the same principles as the double roof formation.

With these figures, you will be able to observe at the bottom of a bearish trend, where you will find two (2) minimums located almost on the same level as if they represented in this place an invisible floor, which confirmed that the price is heading upward trend.

Triple roof:

This figure belongs to the set of repetitive formations that give way to a change in the direction of the price.

It occurs during an uptrend and is characterized by having high reliability at the time of indicating a change in the trend.

The name of this figure is evident by its characteristic shape. It is formed by three (3) peaks located at the same level, but unlike the pattern of the double roof, this one breaks that invisible ceiling which kept them located at the same height, to give an end to the current trend and to give a start to a new different trend.

Therefore when we talk about triple ceiling we refer to a pattern that will give away when the market changes from a bullish to a bearish trend.

Triple floor:

With the help of this figure, you can anticipate the movement and thus evaluate the change that will manifest in the current trend upwards.

If the triple roof pattern was an upward trend and changed to a bearish trend, you will find it in the market as a bearish trend with its (3) peaks located at the same level, forming this an invisible floor which kept them at the same level breaking this to give it the end of the current trend and open the way to the different trend, in this case the uptrend.

By this point, you already know the most important figures that can be found in the market, as well as how to use them to somehow predict a change in.

CHAPTER V:

Indicators

There is a wide variety of indicators that can help you study the movement of the market and, if you are lucky, predict its behavior.

A trading indicator is a graphic that is attached to your trading platform so that it flows parallel to the price or forms part of it.

Its values are born from formulas or mathematical or statistical algorithms applied to a series of prices or volumes, which are reflected in the graph created by the corresponding indicator. Although some have sophisticated names, do not be scared, it only takes a little patience to understand how they work.

Trading indicators inform which direction the market may go, whether it is bullish or bearish; or at each moment indicate the strength of the movement.

The main function of an indicator is to compare the current evolution of the price with its evolution in the past, showing you something that the market is not capable of doing by itself. However, there are other uses such as:

- Pointing out purchases and sales
- Measuring strengths or positions
- Evaluating divergences
- Establishing overbought and oversold states

All this depending on the type of indicator and what you are looking for.

It is important to bear in mind that no indicator is infallible.

In other words, news exists and affect the market drastically, especially the bad ones, so no one can accurately forecast the behavior that the market will take.

Peter Matera

In this regard, you have to perceive the indicators as technical analysis tools that indicate the likelihood of a concrete movement.

Experience is required to read the market correctly since the world of trading is complex and difficult to predict. One tip would be to keep it as simple as possible because often too much information does not translate into an accurate diagnosis.

Do not complicate things too much. Being a trader involves managing the indicators that we feel comfortable with, some ingenuity and even a bit of luck.

• <u>Oscillating Indicators: MACD and RSI</u>

The oscillating indicators, also known as swing traders, reflect the ups and downs that the market suffers, which can serve to stipulate how strong the current trend is and when it will lose its momentum and change its direction.

For example, if it goes too high it is considered to be overbought, where, having acquired many people, the interest will disappear, losing momentum and therefore changing course.

The same happens in the opposite scenario if it goes down a lot, leading to overbooking and increased supply.

As is known, the quotes of assets do not move in a straight line, but moves up and down, creating undulations or oscillations, representing the twists that the dynamism of the market has.

That you take advantage of these cries is the end of the oscillating indicators, developing strategies to identify turning points.

This is achieved by studying the data provided by any of the different types of oscillating indicators, which fluctuate from 0 to 100, being used to detect the entry and exit times of an asset.

Two of the most common oscillating indicators are:

MACD:

It is considered the most known and used trading indicator.

Its name is given by the abbreviations in English of Moving Average Convergence/Divergence, that is, Mobile Media of Convergence and Divergence.

This indicator, created by Gerald Apple at the end of the 70s, has as its main function to be a follower of trends and momentum, fluctuating above and below zero, showing the relationship between two moving averages of prices.

It is common to find it below the movement of prices in graphs, arming according to a series of moving averages and their relation to each other.

Continuing with the previous idea, the MACD is constituted by two parts: the pair of lines, one of them representing the difference between two moving averages and the other one called the signal line; and the MACD histogram.

The first line, the so-called main line, is the subtraction between the exponential moving averages of 12 and 26 intervals.

The average of the 12 bars is considered to be the fast average, being more sensitive with short-term price changes.

On the other hand, the average of the 26 bars is taken as the slow average, being less sensitive to short-term movements, and less noisy to interpret.

The relationship between the two forms the main line, which I recommend painting a little darker to make it stand out.

Its mathematical expression is:

MACD = med (cotiz.12) - med (cotiz.26)

Peter Matera

The signal line is that which results from a moving average calculated from the main line, which is 9 intervals.

This will cross every so often with the main line and its objective is to indicate the best moments to buy or sell. You can use it in two ways:

- One where you buy and sell when both lines intersect
- Other when you buy both when you exceed 0 and sell when they are less than 0.

Its formula is:

Sing = med (MACD9)

Finally, the MACD histogram arises because of the difference between the main line and the signal line.

In this way, it informs you of the distance that exists between the curves that form the two lines.

It is a visually useful bar since in each time lapse it tells you if you are in a bull market or bear market.

This way, in case the bars are above 0, usually in yellow, it means that the bulls send and the trend is likely to continue. However, if the bar changes color and passes to a value below 0, it means that the trend is no longer strong.

RSI:

It was developed by J. Welles Wilder in 1978 and means Relative Strength Index.

It is an indicator that is expressed as a percentage, ranging from 0% to 100%, with 50% being the central or neutral area, and it measures the strength of the price; how fast the value of an asset rises or falls within a certain period of time.

This indicator is represented with a linear graph that changes into oscillations depending on changes in the market.

The RSI points out the overbought and oversold areas of the asset by establishing two fixed lines that serve as limits, traditionally of 30 and 70.

The graph fluctuates the moving average of the RSI, which the further up indicates that the demand is increasing and if it exceeds the upper limit of 70 you would find yourself in an overbought zone, which you can interpret as being at any moment extinguished and become a supply force.

In the opposite case, if the moving average of the RSI decreases, the offer obtains power and being less than 30 you would be in the presence of an oversold scenario.

Following this thread of ideas, if the moving average oscillates around 50, it informs that the forces of demand and supply are relatively identical, that is to say, that there is no marked tendency.

Mathematically speaking it expresses like this:

RSI = 100 - (100/1 + RS)

RS = the average of increases in n periods – the average of decreases in n periods

It was recommended to use the RSI in 14 periods when it was first introduced by Welles Wilder, however, the RSI of 9 and 25 periods have also been well accepted, as well as the use of the limits of 20 and 80, which are considered safer than the standard range.

• <u>Trend indicators:</u>

Unlike oscillating indicators, trend indicators are designed to detect trends in the market, informing you about the direction of price movement.

They help you avoid false signals and predict possible new trends in the market, calculating their values from averages and smoothing price series.

Two examples of them are:

Moving Average:

Abbreviated as MA, is a tool that determines the average price of an asset within a period of time.

- It is used to simplify the evolution of quotes, giving you a clearer picture of the direction of the trend and its strength.
- It is important to emphasize that it is not an indicator that anticipates but reacts by pointing out when a new trend starts or an old trend modifies its direction.

Moving averages are born from various data, classified into 3 types: simple moving average, weighted moving average, and exponential moving average.

The simple moving average is the most used by traders due to its simplicity and contribution of clear buy and sell signals.

This indicator is the arithmetic mean of the last periods. Its disadvantages are that it gives the same importance to both the first and the last day and that only considers the chosen period while the rest isn't taken it into account.

Its mathematical representation is:

SMA = sum of recent closing prices/number of periods

The weighted moving average, on the other hand, is the one that gives more weight to the recent quotes than to the initial ones of the exposed period, reducing the delay that is generated in the simple moving average.

This is obtained by multiplying the oldest period by 1, the penultimate period by 2, and so on until the current period. Then, the sum of the result of these products is divided by the sum of the weights.

Example of the formula for the 3-day period:

WMA_3 = (3 * Quote today + 2 * Quote yesterday + 1 * Quote 2 back) / (3 + 2 + 1)

Finally, the exponential moving average gives greater weight to nearby data and also reacts with speed to changes.

It is good to mention that the old values do not affect it greatly because they disappear with time.

It is represented as:

EMA = (Price today * k) + (Price yesterday * (1 - k)

$k = 2/(number \ of \ days \ in \ the \ period + 1)$

Choosing the ideal extension of the period is not easy and it is advisable to adapt it to market conditions.

A short moving average

Consists of around 5 to 20 days and is more sensitive.

Therefore, it adjusts to prices, allowing you to identify new trends more quickly.

However, it modifies the direction more than usual and may give you erroneous signals.

Peter Matera

A medium-term moving average

Ranges between 20 and 70 days. And long moving average goes from 70 to 200 days, throwing less false signals.

The recommendation is to cover half of the dominant market cycle, that is, if the market cycle is 40 days, the moving average that you should use should be 20 days.

Many traders prefer a moving average that fluctuates between 10 and 20 days but uses the period size that you consider convenient.

Keep in mind that it should never be less than 8 since it loses its function as a trend indicator.

You can use moving averages in several ways.

One is having a single mobile average that provides the buy or sells signal each time it crosses the value of the prices. Another way is that you have two moving averages, one short and one long-term, where your crossing will give you the signal you require.

The tactic is to buy when the quotes cut in ascending order to their moving average and sell when they do so descend.

ADX:

The Directional Movement Index, or Average Directional Movement Index, is an indicator developed by Welles Wilder with the goal of determining the strength of the trend of future price movements, studying the relationship between the difference of the minimum values and maximum prices. It warns you if there is a trend or not in the prices, going from 0 to 100.

An ADX line that goes up detects a trend, either bullish or bearish. When you evaluate your directional movements, you see two fixed lines, directional indicators, named + DI and -DI.

One measures positive upward movements and the other negative downward movements. When + DI grows above -DI it is taken as an indication of purchase. If conversely, -DI grows above + DI, then it looks like a sell signal.

Formula:

$$ADX = MA\ [((+ DI) - (-DI)) / ((+ DI) + (-DI))] * 100$$

Note: If the ADX value is greater than 25, then the trend is strong.

Fibonacci recoil.

Fibonacci retracement is a tool used in trading to forecast probable points of entry or exit within a trend, establishing what is known as supports or resistances. These setbacks are the possibility that the price of an asset will go back considerably compared to the original movement, in other words, to the previous trend.

You can observe it as the fall in price after an uptrend, or the price rebound after a bearish trend. What is sought as such is to calculate the magnitude of the movement already confirmed by quantifying the amplitude or height of the movement divided between the Fibonacci sequency.

Fibonacci was formulated by Leonardo Pisano, an Italian mathematician, around 1200 a.C. It focuses on the sum of the last two consecutive numbers of a repeated sequence of numbers, which continues to infinity and has several curious features.

The first values of the series are: 0, 1, 1, 2, 3, 5, 8, 21, 34, 55, 89, 144, 233, 377, 610, 987, 1.597, 2.584, and so on. This numerical sequence is surprisingly present persistently in nature.

In this way, what is called the Golden Number or Divine Proportion is originated, on the basis that the universal nature tends to be accommodated through harmonic proportions, found in the Fibonacci sequency.

From this appears the Gold Number or Phi: 1.61803 or its inverse 0.681, linked to a myriad of balanced interactions.

This special number together with other ratios that come from it make up the Golden Reason.

These salient ratios are:

- 23.6% (given by the division of a number of the sequence between the third that follows it)
- 38.2% (from the division of one of the numbers between the second that continues
- 68.1% (which is dividing the number between the next one).

In addition, in the analysis of Fibonacci retracements, there is a tendency to add three more levels that, although not calculated as a result of the succession, are formulated from the three previous ratios.

These are 50% (it is the average value between 61.8% and 38.2%); 76.4% (the difference between 38.2% and 23.6% and adding 61.8%); and 100% (corresponding to the level where the impulse or the previous trend began).

Consequently, the first three ratios are those that indicate the backward movement of the previous advance, in which the price has a greater probability of stopping, especially in 61.8% when it coincides with Phi.

If the retracement exceeds 76.4%, you should take it as a prediction of a total change of the current trend.

In turn, the area that goes from 38.2% and 61.8% is often called the Fibonacci Zone.

Having already that, to work with the Fibonacci Recoils you must first draw a vertical line between the two extremes of a strong market movement.

The line is divided into the six ratios already mentioned and adding 161.8%, 261.8% and 423.6%, which indicate the projections or price objectives.

After a rise or fall, prices tend to correct their initial movement returning to previous levels, encountering supports or resistance at or near the Fibonacci ratios.

The theory of this tool can help you as a trader or investor to identify warning signs in the market.

If the price drops to 38.2%, it is said that the trend is strong because it is only the minimum level of setbacks. On the other hand, if it drops to 61.8% it is an indication that the trend is weak and a new one is likely to start.

In this theory, 50% is taken into account, despite not belonging as such to the Fibonacci sequence, because according to the Dow Theory, the averages or trends commonly fall back to half of their previous movement and then rise again.

Among traders, it is popular to expect the price to fall to one of the Fibonacci levels to enter the market and thus achieve an increase in profits. However, to maximize its use it is recommended to use it together with other indicators, such as the MACD and Moving Averages, thus increasing the chances of success.

Keep in mind that, although the Fibonacci sequence describes the harmonious balance of nature, it is not a magic number that will always win you. Fibonacci retracements only show us the levels where the market is expected to find support or resistance, but as volatility increases, its effectiveness decreases. Remember that in trading you need to consider several factors and therefore it is good to use different tools that support the decisions you will make.

At this point, you are already well aware of the tools that can be used to get an accurate analysis, from which you will be able to make a winning strategy later on.

Yet, all the technical and statistical information can be torn apart by the most destructive force of nature, humanity.

The market is nothing but the feelings and investments of millions of men and women who are pursuing profit through its movements, and, are susceptible to feelings towards risk, benefit, and loss.

Get to see them

Now, to close this chapter, here is an image in which you can appreciate the five indicators that we explained above:

1. Moving Average Line

2. Fibonacci Lines

3. MACD

4. RSI

5. ADX

CHAPTER VI:

Correlation analysis, Fundamental, Psychology of Trading.

In this chapter, you will learn about the assets and currencies currently operated, how the market works and volatility and how to interpret and correlate them.

We will also talk a bit about the news and how they manipulate even the most subtle of the markets that seem to have nothing to do with the issue, how to react to them and how to interpret them, do we stay out or do we enter?

We will also touch on the subject of emotions that, in a market that moves mostly money, YOU money, must be studied, understood, observed and managed perfectly to avoid emotional and financial disasters, and mainly, avoid creating an endless cycle of they.

In addition, we will see the emotions we feel most at the time of operating. It may seem that you are facing your poker-faced computer without any pain from seeing a red candle moving, but are you screaming inside?

• <u>List of existing prices of assets and currency pairs.</u>

Forex trading is considered the one with the highest risk index due to the high volatility of most of its peers. On the other hand, the assets tend to have slightly more slight and lateral movements, in the same way, some more than others.

In both cases, we will mention your current prices, but they vary daily and even from one minute to another, so you should not take those prices as guides or stable prices of any product in the stock market.

The assets are divided into:

Raw materials:

These are the materials extracted from nature whose refined product is used to create other goods for later consumption. The most traded commodity CFDs in the world are:

- Oil $ 51.76
- Coffee $ 111.00
- Natural gas $ 4.27
- Gold $ 1229.20
- Silver $ 14.37
- Sugar $ 12.48
- Corn $ 367.75
- Wheat $ 513.15
- Cotton $ 77.87

Actions:

They represent a unit of property or a smaller part of a company.

Also known as securities, they are created when companies divide their shares into so many equal amounts to be sold to investors or shareholders and fluctuate depending on the success or failure of the company in question.

Today, the most commercialized are:

- Amazon.com, Inc. $ 1555.86
- General Motors Company $ 38.03
- Apple Inc. $ 171.53
- Alphabet Inc. (Google) $ 1047.68
- Tesla, Inc. $ 340.79
- Walmart, Inc. $ 95.23

- Industrea Acquisition Corp. $ 10.26
- Campbell Soup Company $ 39.32
- Target Corporation $ 68.55

Stock indices:

These, as we explained in the first chapter, are the sum of market environments, and the most popular ones would be:

- IBEX 35, Spain $ 9091.20
- I.G. Bolsa Madrid, Spain $ 913.46
- Dow 30, United States $ 24551.05
- S & P 500, United States $ 2663.88
- Nasdaq, United States $ 7042.71
- Russell 2000, United States $ 1499.40
- S & P 500 VIX, United States $ 19.45
- S & P / TSX, Canada $ 15015.85
- Bovespa, Brazil $ 85246.79
- Merval, Argentina $ 31550.31

It is important to highlight that, when trading in raw materials, stocks and indices, the schedule of the country of origin of the asset must be respected and the price variations in each one, in addition to the natural fluctuations of the market due to supply and demand, originate due to the political, economic and social situation of the same country.

The currencies are located in pairs in the Forex market.

Each currency is represented by a code of three letters that resemble its name, for example, EUR is Euro, USD is US Dollar, and so we would find the pair of the Euro against the Dollar: EURUSD, EUR/USD, EUR USD or EUR.USD.

Peter Matera

The first currency represents the base currency and the second represents the quote currency. The figure generated in the change represents the amount of the second that is necessary to acquire the first.

So, if the EURUSD is trading at 1.1336, it means that buying 1Euro costs $ 1.13.

The pairs with the largest volume today are:

- EUR / USD Euro vs American Dollar 1.1332
- USD / JPY American Dollar vs. Japanese Yen 113.53
- GBP / USD British Pound vs. American Dollar 1.2819
- USD / CHF American Dollar vs. Swiss Franc 0.9982
- USD / CAD American Dollar vs Canadian Dollar 1.3241
- EUR / JPY Euro vs Japanese Yen 128.66
- AUD / USD Australian Dollar vs American Dollar 0.7228
- NZD / USD New Zealand Dollar vs American Dollar 0.6785
- EUR / GBP Euro vs. British Pound 0.8841
- EUR / CHF Euro vs Swiss Franc 1.1311

The rise or fall in the price of a currency also depends on the economic situation of the most important countries for the market that use it as the main currency, of the political decisions taken by their governments.

It can also reflect the decrease of one in comparison to its counterpart, in the case of the strengthening of the second.

This market is also directly affected by the raw materials and companies that support it.

For example, if the price of oil goes up, this strengthens the currencies of oil-producing countries, that is, in a simple chain of relations: the raw material (oil) increases its value, in the same way, its product does (gasoline), and that is the gasoline that Canada produces to sell to the United States, then the Canadian Dollar (CAD) also rises.

In this case, at the time of a technical analysis we could observe that (for example):

- The USD / CAD chart and other charts in which the Canadian Dollar is the quoted currency are in a bearish trend, or
- The USD / CAD chart and other graphs in which the Canadian Dollar is the quoted currency, slow down its movements and lateralize.

The currencies are usually the assets that react most quickly and volatile to the news and eventualities related to them, policies, natural disasters, raw materials, large corporations, other markets, and other eventualities.

Therefore, in the next section, we will talk about the news and how they have an impact on the price of market assets.

• <u>How does the news affect?</u>

The news, both previously announced and surprise ones affect in a positive or negative way the short, medium and long-term trading.

Having a technical analysis polished, but not being aware of the economic calendar can lead to your operations being reversed by simply opening them at a bad moment.

Regardless of the type of asset with which you operate, you will always be exposed to unexpected news and a change to all your predictions.

Then, the least we can do is to keep abreast of those whose existence we previously know.

There are different types of news that can affect one or more products when going on the air:

Corporations include forecasts

Fines, business results and regulatory changes that may affect a company or several companies belonging to the same sector.

For example, the fraud of the Volkswagen that came to light at the end of 2015 obviously generated outright losses in the shares of that company, but the distrust that generated in the automotive sector came to affect its competitors generating losses in most of them.

Planned news such as press conferences and presentation

Mostly about results of economic indicators that affect the markets to a greater extent.

This affects the exchange of currencies and their prices, although it also affects companies in a certain sector depending on the announced data.

In addition, the changes generated by them tend to affect markets only in the short term.

For example, the speculative net positions in the CFTC's silver, despite being the positions of the traders that exchange in the futures market, indicates the level of confidence that they have in that market, and to give negative results, It would incite another large number of investors to go short, showing weakness on the part of this material and, therefore, affecting its traders.

Institutional or political events

Events such as wars, trade agreements, diplomatic conflicts, leaders' meetings, OPEC announcements and other types of government relations, especially those not previously announced, affect both the different production sectors and the main currencies of the countries involved, even from industries minimally linked with them.

For example, if a telephone company has its factory and distributors in the United States but its parts come from Turkey, and an economic disaster occurs that directly involves the country of origin, the cost of the raw material acquired by the company will be affected, and In turn, the product that you commercialize.

Later on, this would affect the company's share values and therefore its value as an investment asset.

The news at the close of the market

These are the ones that produce the highest volatility in the first minutes of the next opening, generating the GAPs or market jumps that sometimes take ahead any operation left overnight.

Now that you know the types of news, you know how it directly affects companies and currencies related to them.

But, something that you must take into account and study based on past news to know the effect of those that may arise, is the reaction that markets have to news apparently not linked to them.

For example, due to disagreements between OPEC and a country that represents the main oil productions, the coveted liquid begins to be scarce, due to its demand other traders increase their value and as a consequence increases the value of common gasoline, as expected.

But at the same time, the shares of companies dedicated to air transport rise sharply, why? Because the biggest investment made by these companies to provide their services effectively is aimed at the fuel of the aircraft.

This may seem overthought, but it is in this way that the news influences positively or negatively in the market and the different products they offer.

And just as some news may seem irrelevant to the product with which we operate, there are others that may seem of greater importance and don't move the markets because either most investors or large investors ignored it.

Leaving the market will be in a kind of standby without any reaction, or the expected result was so obvious that the market reacted prior to its official publication making its move ahead of time.

There are a lot of traders that operate only in news and get positive results, but the idea is to maintain a harmonious balance between technical and news analysis to avoid anything overlooked, because it is possible to prevent graphic moves with the knowledge of the news and their reactions, but there are also repetitive graphic patterns that are not always backed by news, and their presence can reverse an operation based only on fundamental studies.

In fact, the news can uncover emotions in us that we did not even know we could feel.

Controlling the news is impossible, but our emotions towards them is another story which is what the next section is about.

• **Psychology of trading**

The psychology of trading is the management of emotions around this activity.

Most people seek information about trading because they want to see results, generate more income, and understand the markets or even make a living from trading.

But one detail that many novices overlook is that of emotions, and it turns out to be the most critical of all.

When you start to understand how the stock market works, how it moves and how it relates to your day-to-day life, you want to be part of it.

That initial motivation gives a direct jump to anxiety when you start to operate.

And it is not for anything other than pure human behavior: to want to see immediate results.

You create an account in a broker, you see a couple of graphs, make some lines, look over the economic calendar and open an operation.

Next, you are starting, you feel safe and full of energy, you have studied "a lot" to achieve success as a professional trader, your operation turns green almost immediately, you are filled with pride, your head is inflated and while your ego elevates you, your operation is reversed and you lose your money.

Maybe that story does not necessarily happen to you in the first operations because of something called "beginner's luck" which is nothing more than letting ourselves be guided by that emotion and flying with an ecstasy that makes everything we do at that moment seem like a piece of cake.

But, as you observe and know your emotions you know that you have probably been there. And when anxiety becomes rage and rage to constant frustration, you can end up giving up.

The stock market is a lot of economies, number, and analysis, but it is more psychology than anything else.

A professional trader who knows the numbers and statistics of the company to which he bet his money knows the possibilities, manages his emotions and expects a certain result, he will not take his capital for bad news or comments from a friend or family member.

A professional analyst knows where a graphic is going that is forming a certain pattern or that is treading an important line, so he remains calm at the time of a confirmation or rebound because he knows that three candlesticks do not change the result and he has calculated well the trajectory.

Peter Matera

In both cases, patience must be the rule.

No matter which market you want to invest in, the first thing you should do is keep calm in any operation you open, and learn to analyze what motivates you or what you feel when opening a certain operation.

All markets are volatile, and all are affected by news, governments and large investors, and the first people affected by this are retail investors full of knowledge, but a nervous hand when it comes to operating.

Those who open an operation that will pay off in four hours at least and do not take off the view of the screen for twenty minutes to end up losing patience and closing, although it is in red, are the first to be expelled from the market by himself.

If you have never stopped to observe yourself, it is time to start doing it. With practice, you will find many emotions in a very short time.

Fear to see the operation reverse, greed for increasingly higher profits, with less capital in less time, stress for not being able to control the movement of the pips, joy when the operations come out positive, anger when the opposite happens...

Feeling these emotions in a way similar to that described while operating is perfectly normal, we are not sorcerers, we are traders.

However, sometimes what matters is how you feel before making any decision.

These emotions can affect you positively or negatively in your trading day.

Entering the market with a real account for the first time can generate panic, with joy and optimism can lead you to make bad decisions, with greed can lead you to abuse the leverage, with stress can make you operate without any

100

sense, with anger can make you close for no reason, and all of them can make you lose money.

To enter the market following the heart is something that few recommend.

If you have a well-founded analysis that tells you to go long, but your instinct screams that you do it shortly, it is preferable that you follow the analysis.

Making the mistake of keeping CFDs of shares of a certain company because you remember their golden years is just as dangerous.

It can bring you memorable memories, but if the numbers are red and you keep them for attachment, that company will take more than your memories, your capital.

Be patient. Warren Buffet did not get to where he is in five minutes. No professional trader did.

So, before putting your money in risk, take a moment to reread the strategies that you have already seen, create a plan that suits you, that includes indicators, lines, instruments, assets, schedules and, if possible, a moment of silence and peace of mind before starting to operate.

Take advantage of your demo account to test your plan and refine it as you see what's best for you and what you should change, which indicator is easier to understand, with what level of volatility you feel better working, how are the values of the companies that You evaluated, and when you start, leave your heart out of it.

It is understandable that the market offers you the possibility of using up to five hundred times your capital, but do not leverage in excess.

Use reasonable sizes. Remember that the lower the capital, the lower the level of risk and the less stress for you.

Peter Matera

Start with a couple of operations until you develop better criteria, there will be a point where you leave some open while you go to take a nap because, at that point, you will know that your money is being well spent.

Also, is human to make mistakes. So, don't get carried away by one or another operation that closes badly.

When you are about to panic because a red candle begins to form when you invest in the long term, remember the people who sold their BITCOIN because they would never be worth more than a couple of cents.

Do not be put off! Follow your logic! Yet in the last chapter, we will give you some powerful advice to get yourself together and find real profitability through your portfolio.

CHAPTER VII:

Trading Dos And Don'ts; Trading Strategies That Actually Work.

By this point, you already know most of what is needed to be a professional trader. We have spoken about the basics, where to invest, and the best platform available at the moment to practice and place your investments.

But having a toolbox doesn't mean that you can actually build something, which is why this final chapter is focused on showing you the 7 rules for safe trading, along with three trading strategies that actually show good results.

- ## <u>7 rules for safe trading.</u>

When you open a trading operation risk is always at hand, and there is no such a thing like risk-free investments.

There are several ways to proceed with your operations, several means to get the information about each asset and several moments in which you can enter or get out of the market during each phase.

This way, aiming to reduce the risk, we prepared 7 rules that will guarantee a safer trading operation:

1. Money at risk

This is something that professional traders keep as a mantra, and that has a good reason to be that way.

"Invest only money that you are willing to lose"

Peter Matera

Repeat that to yourself before placing bids or even charging your account. If you are going to invest, the best way to do it is using money that was meant to be for investing.

This way, avoid using the money that you need to keep your daily expenses, the money that you saved to move out or do something else that could compromise your objectivity towards its movement in the market.

2. Use your knowledge

This point goes in two directions, you should always trade in something that is appealing to you.

The reason behind this rule is simple. When trading, you will have to find information about your assets, be always aware of what is happening to them.

If, for example, you opened a buying operation on a sports company shares, and you dislike sports, it will be annoying for you to get overwhelmed with sports information every single day, day after day until the operation closes.

Also, by liking the field in which you are working and even being an expert on it, you will have access to much more information.

Let's make the opposite example, you are an IT manager, you are always surrounded by technology and know exactly how the local market develops, how things work inside an IT company and how news can directly affect your field of work.

This way, you will have a better notion of what is going on news-wise in the technology sector and can use that knowledge to apply a faster response to your operations when news hit.

3. Go with the flow

Going against the flow is the easiest way to lose money in trading, but, what is the flow?

Well, the flow is the major trend of the asset, the one that is visible in the monthly r yearly chart, and the one that has a stronger influence on the price's future.

How do you spot it?

The stronger a trend, the easier to spot, but usually going to your monthly chart and looking to 8 or more candlesticks following a trend is going to be enough for you to know where the price is heading.

In addition to this, you can use the ADX indicator to ensure that the trend is still strong.

On the other hand, you should check all temporalities above the one in which you are going to invest, this way you ensure that your operation won't due to mid-time different trends.

About that last point, the price can be in different directions for each temporality. Said in other words, the trend could be bullish in the monthly chart, but if it isn't strong enough, the weekly and even the daily chart can be going down.

In this scenario, the safer thing to do is to analyze the chart toughly aiming to the possible pricing outcomes.

4. Cut off the operation if the trend goes back

A common mistake for beginners is to "hope" that the price goes back in track toward the path that their analysis predicted.

This is a great way to lose money. If you ever see a return pattern showing off with strength, and then you see that the volumes aim to follow that change, there is nothing that you can do to take things back.

Therefore, in order to not lose the whole operation, it is better for you to retreat with little loss.

5. Never use all your money at once

We mean it, never open one or several positions using all the money in your account.

This will be a great risk and if you do not calculate well it could mean losing all your money in the blink of an eye.

The best advice is to always trade with half of your investing money, this allows you to keep a backup plan in case that your operations go wrong.

Which takes us to rule number six.

6. "Don't put all your eggs in the same basket"

You probably heard that before right?

Let's make an example of the reasons why. Imagine that you were a trader in 2015 –And keep in mind the Volkswagen case-, now, imagine that your portfolio had, not only Volkswagen but GM, Ford, Peugeot, Fiat and all sort of vehicle industry assets.

You were following rule number two, right, but since all of the above, especially the European marks, lost value drastically by the fourth quarter of that year, your losses would have been incredible.

Usually, it is important to diversify your assets, USD and OIL go in different directions all the time, which mean that if one falls you can still get money from the operations made in the other.

This being said, try to balance diversification with the rule number two, and aim to have a portfolio that reflects you and your personal tastes.

7. Keep your heart out of it!

This is basically the most important rule of trading. The hardest thing to do is to always be rational when your money is at stake, but making decisions in cold is by far the best option, especially when the market shows uncertainty.

Cold thinking will allow you to evaluate your options better and will help you decide whether if you want to drop an operation or the trend is going to be back to where you need it to go.

Either way, the psychology of trading has an incredible impact on your results, which is where most traders end giving up to the market.

This is why, in the end, all the other six rules help you following this one:

- Placing only money that you can lose, will prevent you from falling in despair.
- Opening positions in a field or industry that you like and know, will avoid you from feeling incertitude about the effect of news or markets positions.
- Going with the flow will grant you extra security, keeping you away from rushing changes in the market.
- Closing your negative operation on time will keep you from getting too attached with an asset.

- Having a backup of about the 50% of your investment capital will make you feel safe, therefore allowing you to keep the mind clear if any operation backfires.
- And finally, distributing the weight of your investments along a diversified portfolio will grant you more opportunities to get income from different sources, thus making it easy for you to recover any loss.

By following these rules you will have a safer travel in every operation that you open, regardless of the position you play and the possibilities in which the price may move.

But a strategy is always needed in order to get real profits, which is why in the next section we are going to explain three simple but unbreakable strategies that traders use to increase their income.

• <u>Strategies for ensuring profitable operations</u>

First of all, it is important to recall the fact that no strategy is flawless, trading means a risk regardless of how prepared you are when opening a position, and in the end, if a strategy poses 70-80% of success rate, any professional trader will qualify it as reliable.

Before testing a strategy with real money, it is extremely important to evaluate it in a demo account and perform a full backtesting.

Currently, most Forex brokers allow you to open accounts for free, as we explained in previous chapters.

Use the trading strategy that best suits your style and personality.

For example, if a trader by his temperament does not have a lot of patience to get results, it is not convenient to use strategies that require hours or even days to produce the expected benefits.

It is not advisable for you to focus on a single trading strategy.

If a trading system does not produce good results during a given period, it is best to replace it with a more appropriate one or wait for the market to provide better conditions for its application.

Flexibility is the key to profitability when we speak of trading.

On the other hand, having a list of strategies is a better idea.

A specific strategy can be fit for different moments and stages of the market, allowing you to get more profitable results in different moments.

If you have several proven and profitable trading systems, you will be able to adapt to the different changes that take place in the market and in the same way you will be able to obtain benefits regardless of whether the trend goes up or down.

Three profitable quick strategies

These three quick strategies will follow up to give you extra opportunities and are usually reliable for investing in FOREX markets.

"Hammer and hung man" Strategy:

The Hammer and hung man bar is a basic element of the way of the Forex market. It has a very high accuracy rate in the trend markets and especially when they occur in a confluent level.

Hammer and hung man that occur at significant levels of support and resistance are generally very accurate indicators of a change in the tendency.

Peter Matera

These can be taken as counter-trend as well, provided that they are very well defined and stand out significantly from the surrounding price bars, indicating that a strong rejection has occurred

To operate with them, use preferably the daily chart or below since this type of patterns stands out for quick turnaround changes.

False break Strategy:

The false break means that there is not going to be a change in the market. This trading strategy is another price action configuration to ask for.

It indicates the rejection of an important level within the market. Many times the market will seem to be headed in one direction and then reverse, sucking all the amateurs or novices to the extent that professionals push the price back in the opposite direction.

The false break take's place when the tendency seems to continue with less strength and the shadow of a candle near a resistance in bullish trends or a support in the bearish ones manages to break such line.

In addition, the shadow that breaks the line should be long, of about 1.5 or 2 times the length of the body, and in all cases be following a candle of the same color.

This way, it feels as if the trend change, but will ultimately follow its way for a longer period of time.

The false break pattern consists essentially of an internal bar followed by a false break of that internal bar and then a closing again within its range.

Your input should be activated when the price moves up again beyond the height of the internal bar.

110

The roller-coaster strategy

Remember when we spoke earlier about following the major trend? There is a whole strategy based on that, which we will explain ahead, step by step:

Note: Apply this strategy only in 4H or below charts, keep in mind that you will have to be aware of every movement of the market and the longer the periods the most time you will have to be operating.

Note 2: *This is, by all means, a high-risk strategy and should be accompanied with real analysis all the time to avoid a rise in the odds of backfiring.*

1. Confirm the major trend in the monthly chart and make sure that it has enough strength to keep going for a while by using the ADX indicator.
2. Repeat the previous process in weekly and daily charts, always confirming that they all follow the same direction. The most temporalities going the same way, the safer your operation will be.
3. When you finish reviewing the trends in the higher chart temporalities, and if they all go in the same direction −Or at least the monthly, weekly and daily chart do-, you are almost ready to operate.
4. Check out the news, make sure that nothing coming on today or in the past few days can impact the price of your asset in any way and much less cause a change in the current trend.
5. Enter the market in favor of your major trend, but always when the previous movement has gone in the opposite direction. This way, if the major trend is a strong bullish one, you will open a buying position when one or two red candles appear.
6. Then, as soon as the price goes back up, you will close the operation, earning a few pips for each movement.

Keep in mind that moving in 4H charts or below, means that the pips are going to be fewer than in mid or long-term operations, for this reason, the risk is greater in this type of strategy as you will be forced to leverage or trade with high quantities of money in order to see a real benefit from it.

Using a 50:1 or 100:1 leverage is totally acceptable for this scenario. But don't leave it to be as simple as it sounds or you will literally pay for it.

Always keep in mind these rules then roller-coasting:

- **Be aware of trend changing patterns**
- **Be aware of the volume, if there are more traders against the major trend in one temporality you will find that it could take more time than the expected to get your line back in green.**
- **Do not, by any means leave an operation open under this strategy.**
- **Do this only in assets that you have already analyzed thoroughly**

With all these tools you are now ready to start trading, keep in mind that the best strategy will always be to follow an intense analysis; check out the news and keep your charts dirty –As for having your major indicators and lines draw- which will allow you to have a better perspective of your asset.

CONCLUSION

In the end, you already know all that is necessary to begin your journey as a trader. In this regard we have been through the basics in chapter one, getting to speak about the types of assets available in the market, and how they work.

Then, we passed through how the stock market works, the times and schedules in which you can and should operate and how each market opens and closes affecting the assets disposed of in its region.

Later on, the brokers, how to choose an online broker and why —in which we recommended AVAtrade and FX as reliable options-

On chapter two we talked about the movement of the price and how to calculate your earnings, the desired leverage, and its risks, and finally the MT4 platform, which is going to be your best ally covering all the aspects and tools that you can use as a trader.

Next, on the third chapter, we spoke about the technical analysis, temporalities, Japanese candlesticks, and their patterns, as well as the lines that you can draw in your chart to keep track of the historical price movements.

Then we explained the phases of the market, and which type of operation you can pursue in every one of them, followed by technical patterns and their explanation in the fourth chapter.

Knowing what the patterns mean when they will show a continuity or a devolution of the current trend, is something that you will find useful in every operation that you open, as for it is the best way to know when to get in or out of the market.

But patterns still need confirmation, so, in chapter five we spoke about the statistic indicators, MACD, RSI, Moving Averages, ADX, and Fibonacci recoils, which allow you to clear out any doubt about the strength of the price and the current trend on the chart. Thus making it easy to spot future changes.

In chapter six, we got to the human side of trading, and show you how the price is affected by the news and human emotions driven in masses by traders and investors worldwide.

And finally, we got you three To-Go strategies that can be used for quick operations, each one riskier than the other, but all three of them useful if you are willing to risk and profit from a trading operation.

Keep in mind the rules, always analyze the market before placing your money and above all remember to operate cold minded.